EFFICIENT AND EFFECTIVE RESEARCH

A toolkit for research students and developing researchers

Best wishes

Chad Perry

14 Nov 13

CHAD PERRY

© AIB Publications Pty Ltd 2012
First published 2013

Except as provided by the Copyright Act 1968, no part of this publication may be reproduced, stored or transmitted in any form, or by any means, without prior permission in writing from the publisher. Enquiries concerning these terms should be addressed to AIB Publications.

AIB Publications Pty Ltd
27 Currie Street
Adelaide SA 5000
Australia

National Library of Australia Cataloguing-in-Publication entry:

Author:	Perry, Chad, author
Title:	Efficient and effective research: a toolkit for research students and developing researchers / Chad Perry.
ISBN:	9780987372116 (paperback)
Subjects:	Research--Methodology. Action research. Research--Study and teaching. Social sciences--Research. Academic writing.
Dewey Number:	001.42
ISBN:	978-0-9873721-1-6

Design and formatting by Barbara Velasco (Papel Papel)
Printed and bound by Lightning Source

CONTENTS

Introduction

PART A
Efficient research: how to write a thesis and journal articles   01

    CHAPTER 1 A structured approach to presenting theses   03
    Abstract   03
    1 Introduction   03
    2 Basics of structure and style   07
        2.1 Perspectives on the overall structure   07
        2.2 Style used throughout the thesis   14
        2.3 Chunkiness in a thesis   20
    3 Details of chapters and their sections   22
        3.1 Chapter 1 Introduction   22
        3.2 Chapter 2 Research issues   32
        3.3 Chapter 3 Methodology   43
        3.4 Chapter 4 Analysis of data   49
        3.5 Chapter 5 Conclusions and implications   55
    4 Conclusion   66
    Appendix A
    A research proposal structure keyed to the thesis structure   66
    Appendix B
    Types of questions an examiner might ask themself   72
    Acknowledgements   73

    CHAPTER 2 Comprehensive processes of efficient article writing   75
    Abstract   75
    Introduction   75
    Targeting an article's readers   77
    Getting read and cited   83
    Writing—structure and style   88
    Redrafting, sending off and revising   91
    Conclusion   96
    Acknowledgements   97

PART B
Effective research: how to do case, interview and action research — 99

CHAPTER 3 How to do case research: a comprehensive framework for modern researchers — 101
Abstract — 101
Introduction — 101
Appropriateness of the realism paradigm — 103
Systematic case research — 107
    Steps 1 and 2: The research problem and its research issues — 107
    Step 3: Identifying a case and their number — 109
    Step 4: Multiple sources of evidence, including interviews collected over two stages — 112
    Step 5: Quality of the research — 116
    Step 6: Data analysis — 116
    Step 7: Analytic generalisation — 119
Implications for research programs — 120
Conclusion — 122
Acknowledgements — 123

CHAPTER 4 How to do (convergent) interviewing: a methodology to start a research project — 125
Abstract — 125
Introduction — 125
Implementing the convergent interviewing methodology — 126
A comparison of convergent interviewing with alternative methodologies — 139
Strengths and limitations of the convergent interviewing technique — 142
Establishing the validity and reliability of convergent interviewing research — 143
Conclusion — 146
Acknowledgements — 146

CHAPTER 5 How to do action research and report it for an academic audience   147
Abstract   147
Introduction   147
Four paradigms   150
Action research is a blend of two paradigms   155
Criteria for judging the quality of action research projects   163
Conclusion   164
Acknowledgements   173

References   175

Index   193

ABOUT THE AUTHOR

Chad Perry had been a Professor of Marketing at two Australian universities before he semi-retired in 2003. Since then, he has been the chair of the Academic Board and is Emeritus Professor at the Australian Institute of Business (AIB), the only private business school in Australia that can grant DBA and PhD qualifications. He led the development of AIB's academic processes and is currently refining supervision practices.

Chad has supervised an extraordinary number of postgraduate research students (who have completed more than 44 doctorates, and 23 masters and honours degrees) and the Department of Marketing that he previously headed had one of the largest Marketing PhD programs in Australia (measured by graduates per year), if not the largest.

He has written or co-written three textbooks, sixteen book chapters and more than 70 refereed journal articles and 40 conference papers, including articles published in international journals. As a result, he has almost 4000 citations in Scholar Google.

He has been invited to present more than 100 research seminars at more than 30 universities in Australia, New Zealand, Ireland, England, Scotland, Northern Ireland, Austria, Canada, Malaysia, Hong Kong, Macau, Sri Lanka and the Philippines. He has also presented management development workshops in Africa, Asia, Papua New Guinea, the United Kingdom and Australia, as well as doing occasional management consulting projects in some of those countries.

INTRODUCTION

This book has two parts. Part A is aimed at all research students writing a thesis and/or journal articles. That first part is about how to write a thesis and a journal article in an efficient way, and it can be used by all researchers whether they are quantitative or qualitative researchers. In turn, Part B focusses on the effective research done by qualitative researchers who use case, interview or action research methodologies.

Most types of research can be a very creative and autonomous way of earning a living. I remember how, one morning years ago, I was driving to a researcher's lecture and realized no one else knew where I was, or what I was doing—I myself had made the decision to go because I was fascinated by the topic. A wonderful feeling! And happy memories of writing articles with colleagues from around the world keep flooding back.

Part A: Efficient Research. This joy of doing research begins with writing a thesis and journal articles, and that is what Part A is about. Learning to be a researcher can be hard work. Doing a PhD is so arduous that it can be as memorable a process in your professional life as getting married is in your personal life. And then there are the agonies of having an article rejected by a journal after you have worked on it for months or years. Researchers rarely talk about these rejections like they talk about their acceptances, just as investors rarely talk about their stock market losses and talk only about their wins. But 90 percent of researchers have to deal with rejections of their articles. Moreover, the demands on a researcher are increasing in an internationalising world, with the publication of various rankings of departments, universities and journals affecting the reputation of a researcher's department and university (and thus the researcher's career). Clearly, researchers have to become more efficient, producing their quality doctorate and articles more quickly.

So Part A of this book aims to provide guidance about thesis and journal article writing, for starting and developing researchers. I hope it makes your work more efficient, whether the research uses quantitative or qualitative data. It provides guidance about efficiency—how to work on the things that matter in a focussed way. It is based on the extant literature, my experience and help from the experts I acknowledge at the end of each chapter.

The first chapter is about presenting a research thesis such as a doctoral thesis (Perry 1998, 2012). A doctorate is the peak training experience for academics and senior managers. The chapter outlines a structured way of presenting a dissertation that has been proven around the world, including around 44 doctoral theses that I have supervised at Australian universities and the Australian Institute of Business. The approach provides training for later research work; and it inhibits inefficient thesis writing that squanders taxpayers' and/or the candidate's funds, wastes supervisors' time and risks the health, careers and families of candidates. Indications of its success are that Googling "chad perry a structured approach for presenting theses" produces over 140 000 hits; my previous article about it is the most-cited article ever published in Australia and New Zealand's top marketing journal; and two senior managers recently used it to efficiently and effectively complete their part-time doctorate within a short 12 months. This first chapter addresses the problem: how should a postgraduate research student in marketing or a similar field (and his or her supervisor) present the thesis? The structure developed provides a starting point for understanding what a thesis should set out to achieve, and also provides a basis for communication between a student and his or her supervisor. Firstly, criteria for judging a doctoral thesis are reviewed and justification for its structure is provided. Then writing style is considered. Finally, each of the five 'chapters' and their sub-sections are described: introduction, literature review, methodology, analysis of data, and conclusions and implications. Appendices of this chapter cover proposals and examination criteria.

The book's first chapter about writing a thesis is direct preparation for writing articles for academic journals during or after the research degree candidature, and so writing journal articles is the second chapter's topic. Writing journal articles is an essential skill for academics and other researchers. Even academics who love teaching more than research have to be able to write about their experiences for educator's journals and for conferences; these articles will allow other, teaching-oriented academics to improve their practices. This second chapter introduces the core principles involved in writing an article (and conference paper), based on the literature about that skill. The chapter's theme is that article writing is a collaborative craft and not a mysterious art—it is the craft of conversation. Writing the first draft of an article may take two or so days; however, planning and collecting data with colleagues beforehand, and writing a draft table of contents, and then re-drafting it many times and revising it after a journal's reviewers have looked at it, will all take many, many months. Then the joy of acceptance into a conversation will probably come. The chapter covers four parts: targeting an article's readers; getting read and cited; writing—structure and style; and redrafting, sending off and revising.

Part B: Effective Research. Part B of this book concentrates on the three common qualitative methodologies of case, interview and action research. Much academic research is irrelevant to real world practitioners, but this part is about three methodologies that are effective at solving practical research problems. That much academic research from most business schools is ineffective is acknowledged in popular magazines and academic journals. Most of this mainstream research is the highly quantitative, theory-testing type hardly ever read by real-world managers (*The Economist* 2007):

> AACSB International, the most widely recognised global accrediting agency for business schools, announced it would consider changing the way it evaluates research.... Most of the research is highly quantitative, hypothesis-driven and esoteric. As a result, it is almost universally unread by real-world managers.

Moreover, academic research is itself finding that most business school research is ineffective, as pointed out in the sections about paradigms in Chapters 4 and 5 (O'Brien et al. 2010). Even some senior academics acknowledge this fact (Matchett 2010).

So this book is about three methodologies that are not this highly quantitative, theory-testing type: they are case, interview and action research. Each of the three can be used to effectively build social science theories about the complex, real-world problems faced by people interacting with each other and possibly changing their views as they do so.

The first chapter provides a modern framework for case researchers that will allow them to do efficient as well as effective research. Case research is often used because it handles multiple sources of evidence that can be collected in many ways that could help the development of professionals in fields such as management, marketing and education, and help solve practical problems those professionals face. My early article about it has been very well-cited (Perry 1998b).

The second chapter of Part B covers the methodology of interviewing, and of convergent interviewing in particular. Convergent interviewing is a very efficient way of analysing interview data so that interviews focus on key issues, and is especially useful at the start of a research project.

The final chapter is about doing research that covers more than one scientific paradigm. It uses the example of two-paradigm research: action research within the critical theory paradigm, and reports about that research within the realism paradigm. I remember one candidate had been struggling for many long years to turn a worthwhile action research project about change in one firm into a PhD thesis. He listened to a seminar about this final chapter and said, 'Scales fell from my eyes'.

I hope Part B can help those of you who are willing to try one or more of these effective methodologies.

Acknowledgements and dedication. Whether you get help from Part A or B or both parts, I hope you enjoy your research career. I enjoyed most of my career because I worked with so many kind colleagues and supervised so many clever research candidates. I have tried to acknowledge them all at the end of each chapter, and affirm my respect, affection and thanks for them all here, too. And I am grateful that I was given an opportunity to refine the three methodologies and to report them in this book by the niche business school, the Australian Institute of Business. Thank you to you all.

Chad Perry

25 February 2013

PART A

EFFICIENT RESEARCH:
HOW TO WRITE A THESIS AND JOURNAL ARTICLES

CHAPTER 1

A STRUCTURED APPROACH TO PRESENTING THESES:
NOTES FOR CANDIDATES AND THEIR SUPERVISORS

ABSTRACT

This chapter addresses the problem: how should a postgraduate research candidate in management, marketing or a similar field (and his or her supervisor) present the thesis? The structure developed provides a starting point for understanding what a thesis should achieve, and provides a basis for communication between a candidate and their supervisor. Firstly, criteria for judging a PhD thesis are reviewed and justification for its structure is provided. Then writing style is considered. Finally, each of the five 'chapters' and their sections are described: introduction, literature review, methodology, analysis of data, and conclusions and implications.

For acknowledgements and thanks, please refer to the end of this chapter.

1 INTRODUCTION

Doing doctoral research is important because it is the entrance gate into an academic or research career, or the identity card of modern senior managers. All this research must be recorded in a thesis. This note outlines a structure for a PhD or DBA thesis (and possibly a Master's or honours thesis), and is written for candidates doing both quantitative and qualitative research in management, marketing or other professional fields; indeed, many candidates in many other disciplines have used it.

That is, this book chapter addresses the problem: ***How should postgraduate research candidates and their supervisors present the thesis?*** The structure's five chapters are summarised in Table 1. Other writers have provided general procedures for the many parts of the PhD research process (for example, Phillips & Pugh 2000), but these notes concentrate on the thesis itself and do so more comprehensively and with more examples than many other writers do.

Essentially, I argue that a thesis should follow certain style conventions and have five sections: introduction, literature review, methodology, analysis of data, and conclusions and implications. Following this structure and carefully using a standard style will make the thesis match the expectations of most examiners and provide training for much later research work.

This book's chapter's problem is important for postgraduate research candidates. Many universities provide little guidance to candidates, prompting the criticism that, at one university, 'the conditions for the award of degrees in the Graduate Study section of the calendar give more precise information on the size of the paper to be used and the margins to be left on each side of the sheet than on the university's understanding of what a thesis is' (Massingham 1984, p. 15). By using the structure developed below, a candidate will ensure his or her thesis demonstrates the core requirements of a doctoral thesis (Moses 1985):

- a distinct contribution to a body of knowledge through an original investigation or testing of ideas, worthy in part of publication (see a thesis' Chapter 5 below)
- competence in research processes, including an understanding of, and competence in, appropriate research techniques and an ability to report research (see Chapters 3 and 4, plus the whole report format)
- mastery of a body of knowledge, including an ability to make critical use of published work and source materials (see Chapter 2) with an appreciation of the relationship of the special theme to the wider field of knowledge (see Chapters 2 and 5).

By the way, all candidates should ask to see a copy of their faculty's or university's letter that is sent to examiners, to determine the priorities of their faculty/university for the three criteria above and if the faculty has additional criteria (Nightingale 1992); and ask for copies of previous examiners' reports, too. But some examiners may not bother to look at your faculty/university's letter to them (Mullins & Kiley 2002) and so you should be aware of the common issues that all examiners may ask themselves about—some example ones are in Appendix B.

This book's chapter has two main parts. The first part introduces the five 'section' or 'chapter' structure, justifies possible changes to it and considers writing style. In the second part, each of the five chapters of a thesis and their sections are described in some detail: introduction, literature review, methodology, analysis of data, and conclusions and implications.

Table 1 — Example table of contents of a structured thesis

Title page Abstract (with keywords) Table of contents List of tables List of figures Abbreviations Statement of original authorship Acknowledgments	
1	Introduction
1.1	Background to the research
1.2	Research problem, propositions/hypotheses/research issues and contributions
1.3	Justification for the research
1.4	Methodology
1.5	Outline of the report
1.6	Definitions
1.7	Delimitations of scope and key assumptions, and their justifications
1.8	Conclusion
2	Research issues (Sections 2.3 and 2.4 might be allotted a chapter to themselves in a PhD or DBA thesis)
2.1	Introduction
2.2	(Parent theories and classification models)
2.3	(Research problem theory: analytical, conceptual frameworks and related research issues or propositions/hypotheses) (this section sometimes has its own chapter)
2.4	Conclusion
3	Methodology (there may be separate chapters for the different methodologies of stages one and two of a PhD or DBA thesis)
3.1	Introduction
3.2	Justification for the paradigm and methodology
3.3	(Research procedures)
3.4	Ethical considerations
3.5	Conclusion

Table 1 — Example table of contents of a structured thesis (contd)

4		Analysis of data (this chapter usually refers to the analysis of the major stage of the research project)
4.1		Introduction
4.2		Subjects
4.3		(Patterns of data for each research issue or hypothesis)
4.4		Conclusion
5		Conclusions and implications
5.1		Introduction
5.2		Conclusions about each research issue or proposition
5.3		Conclusions about the research problem
5.4		Implications for theory
5.5		Implications for policy and practice
5.5.1		Private sector managers
5.5.2		Public sector policy analysts and managers
6.6		Limitations (this section is sometimes combined with the next one)
6.7		Further research
6.8		Conclusion
References		
Appendices		

Delimitations. The structured approach may be delimited to postgraduate theses in management, marketing and other professional areas that involve quantitative and qualitative methodologies. That is, the structure may not be appropriate for theses in other areas or for theses using unusual methodologies such as historical research designs or grounded theory. Moreover, the structure is a starting point for thinking about how to present a thesis rather than the only structure that can be adopted, and so it is not meant to inhibit the creativity of postgraduate researchers. Another delimitation of the approach is that it is restricted to presenting the *final* version of the thesis. And so this book chapter does not address the techniques of actually writing a thesis and or imply that the issues of each thesis chapter have to be addressed by the candidate in the order shown.

For example, the research issues/propositions/hypotheses at the end of a thesis Chapter 2 are meant to *appear* to be developed as the chapter progresses, but the candidate might have a well-developed idea of what they will be *before* they start to write the chapter. For another example, the methodology of Chapter 3 must *appear* to have been selected because it was appropriate for the research problem identified and carefully justified in Chapter 1, but the candidate may have actually selected the methodology very early in their candidature and then developed an appropriate research problem and justified it. Moreover, after a candidate has sketched out a draft table of contents for each chapter, they should begin writing the 'easiest parts' of the thesis first, whatever those parts are—but usually introductions to chapters are the last to be written (Phillips & Pugh 2000, p. 71). But bear in mind that the research problem, delimitations and research gaps in the literature must be drafted and written down before other parts of the thesis can be written, and that Section 1.1 is often one of the last to be written. Nor is this structure meant to be the format for a doctoral candidate's research proposal—a proposal format that is related to this structure is provided in Appendix A.

2 BASICS OF STRUCTURE AND STYLE

Before each of the five chapters of a thesis is described in detail, the overall structure of a thesis needs to be established and some issues of style in all the chapters need to be covered.

2.1 PERSPECTIVES ON THE OVERALL STRUCTURE

A five-chapter structure can be used to effectively present a thesis, and it is summarised in Figure 1. As you read below, remember that a thesis can actually have more than five 'chapters', as discussed above and below, and in Table 1. Thus the term 'chapter' is used in this book in a generic sense; perhaps 'section' could have been used rather than 'chapter', but doing so may have been confusing because there are 'sections' within each 'chapter'.

Figure 1 — Model of the chapters of a thesis

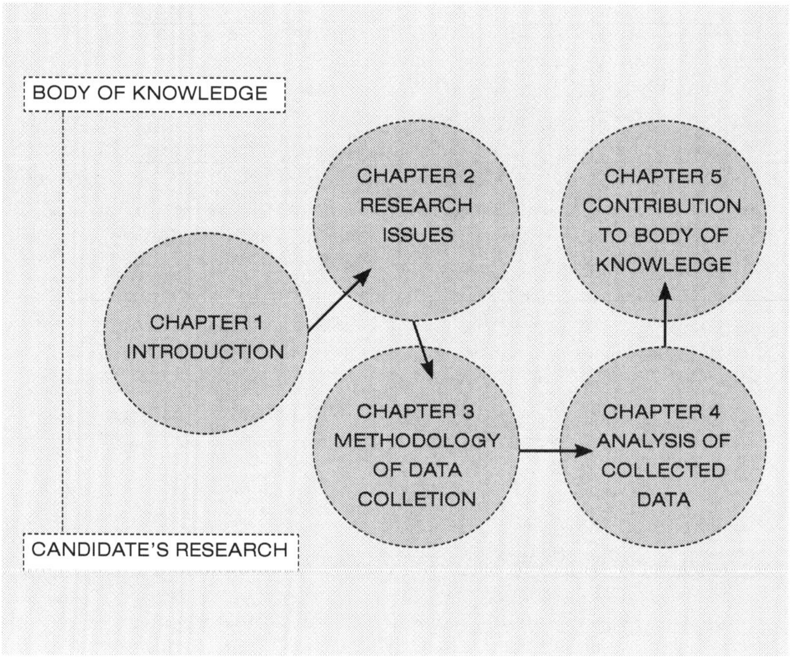

[Figure: Diagram showing BODY OF KNOWLEDGE and CANDIDATE'S RESEARCH regions. CHAPTER 1 INTRODUCTION connects to CHAPTER 2 RESEARCH ISSUES, which connects to CHAPTER 3 METHODOLOGY OF DATA COLLETION, which connects to CHAPTER 4 ANALYSIS OF COLLECTED DATA, which connects to CHAPTER 5 CONTRIBUTION TO BODY OF KNOWLEDGE.]

In brief, the thesis should have a *unified* structure (Easterby-Smith et al. 2008). Firstly, Chapter 1 introduces the core research problem and then 'sets the scene' and outlines the path that the examiner will travel towards the thesis' conclusion. The research itself is described in Chapters 2 to 5, that is, Chapters 2 to 5 cover:

- the research problem and research issues/propositions/ hypotheses arising from the body of knowledge developed during previous research (Chapter 2)
- methods used in this research to collect data about the hypotheses/research issues (Chapter 3)
- results of applying those methods in this research (Chapter 4)
- conclusions about the research issues/propositions/hypotheses and research problem based on the results of Chapter 4,

including their place in the body of knowledge outlined previously in Chapter 2 (Chapter 5).

Incidentally, having numbers in the headings of each section and subsections of the thesis, as shown in Table 1, will help to make the large thesis appear organised and facilitate cross-referencing between sections and subsections. However, some supervisors may prefer a candidate to use headings without numbers, because articles in many journals do not have headings with numbers. But articles are far shorter than theses, and so I prefer to include an explicit skeleton in the form of numbered sections and subsections to carry the extra weight of a thesis.

Justification of the structured approach. This five-chapter structure can be justified. Firstly, the structure is unified and focussed on solving the one research problem. Thus it addresses the major fault of postgraduate theses in Nightingales' (1984) survey of 139 examiners' reports because it clearly addresses those examiners' difficulty in discerning what was the 'thesis of the thesis'? Nightingale concluded that unity and focus depend on supervisors emphasising 'throughout students' candidacies that they are striving in the thesis to communicate one big idea' (Nightingale 1984, p. 174). That one big idea is the *research problem* stated on page 1 or 2 of the thesis and explicitly solved in Chapter 5. Other writers support this need for an over-arching research problem. Easterby-Smith et al. (2008) emphasised the importance of consistency in a PhD thesis; Phillips and Pugh (2000, p. 42) confirmed that a thesis must have a 'thesis' or a 'position'; and Lindsay (1995, pp. 104, 105) insisted that 'the unifying hypothesis ... the purpose of the thesis must be clear from the very beginning'.

There are six other justifications for the structure:

- The structure carefully addresses each of the 31 requirements of an Australian PhD thesis outlined by the authoritative Higher Education Research and Development Society of Australia (Moses 1985, pp. 32–34).
- The structure is explicitly or implicitly followed by many writers of articles in top tier academic journals such as *The Academy of Management Journal* and *Strategic Management Journal*, and so candidates learn skills required by reviewers of those journals while writing their thesis. That is, it trains PhD candidates in how to write journal articles (how articles are written are in this book's Chapter 2; Carson, Gilmore & Perry 2006; Perry, Carson & Gilmore 2003).

The linkages between a thesis and an article are:

THESIS	ARTICLE
parent theories 1 and 2 in Chapter 2	paragraphs 2 and 3
justification in Section 1.3	paragraph 4
research problem theory of Section 2.3	Literature review section
methodology of Chapter 3	Methodology section
data analysis of Chapter 4	Findings section
conclusions in Sections 5.2 and 5.3	Discussion section
implications of Sections 5.4 and 5.5	Implications section

- The structure is based on the established literature about PhD research, for example, Phillips and Pugh (2000), and my own article about it is the most-cited article ever published in Australia's top marketing journal (Perry 1998a).
- The structure has been followed by many PhD, DBA and Masters theses at Australian and overseas universities with no or negligible revisions (including 44 doctoral students of my own)—indeed, Googling 'Chad Perry a structured approach to presenting theses' produces more than 140 000 results; and I have many unsolicited 'thank you' emails from people around the world whom I have not met but who have used the structure for their doctorates (it was given to them by their supervisor or peers, or downloaded from the Internet).
- The structure is why I have been invited to present seminars about it at more than 30 universities in Australia, New Zealand, Ireland, England, Scotland, Northern Ireland, Austria, Canada, Malaysia, Hong Kong, Macau, Sri Lanka and the Philippines.

In brief, the structure provides a mechanism to shorten the time taken to complete a postgraduate degree like a PhD, by reducing the time wasted by candidates on unnecessary tasks or on trying to demystify the thesis-writing process; and so this structure *inhibits* inefficient thesis writing that squanders taxpayers' funds, wastes supervisors' time and risks the health, careers and families of candidates.

Justified changes to the structure. Some changes to the five-chapter structure could be justified. For example, a candidate may find it convenient to expand the number of chapters to six or seven because of unusual characteristics of the analysis in their research; for example, a PhD might consist of two stages: some qualitative research reported in Chapters 3 and 4 of the thesis described below, which is then followed by some quantitative research in Chapters 5 and 6 to refine the initial findings reported in Chapters 3 and 4; the Chapter 5 described below would then become Chapter 7.

In addition, PhD theses at universities that allow large word counts may have extra chapters to contain the extended reviews of bodies of knowledge in those huge theses. I am thinking here of those universities which allow a PhD thesis to rise from the minimum length of about 50 000 to 60 000 words (Phillips & Pugh 2000, p. 54); through the 70 000 to 80 000 words preferred by many examiners; up to the upper limit of 100 000 words specified by some established universities like the University of Queensland. So, in some theses, the five chapters may become five *sections* with one or more chapters within each of them, but the principles of the structured approach should remain.

In brief, the five-chapter structure has some limitations but it also has many benefits for candidates learning the basics of their research craft and beginning their research career, as well as for a busy supervisor who has had little training in research writing or supervision. The structure provides a starting point for understanding what a thesis should set out to achieve, and also provides a basis for communication between a candidate and his or her supervisor. Indeed, with this tested and proven structure, candidates can focus on being creative in their research and not dissipate their creative energies on inventing another structure.

Moreover, with these guidelines for chapter content and construction, it is possible to plan a postgraduate research project along the lines of Tables 2, 3 and 4. As a rough rule of thumb, a thesis' five chapters have these respective percentages of the thesis' words: 6, 34, 18, 22 and 20 percent. The rule of thumb percentages are slightly different from these if a thesis has *two stages* of data collection rather than just the one stage that can be neatly described in a five chapter thesis. In this circumstance, Chapters 3 and 4 would be devoted to the two stages of methodology. Rule of thumb percentages for such a six chapter thesis are about 6, 33, 11, 17, 20 and 13 percent. Using these approximate percentages, a candidate could plan the approximate time and pages for any chapter. For example, a typical, two-stage PhD thesis of 65 000 or so words done in 27 months might look like Table 2, and a one-stage DBA thesis of 50 000 words done in 27 months might look like Table 4. Tables 2, 3 and 4 are merely examples and are not templates for every thesis, because each research project must do whatever is required to solve its own, justified research problem. The tables measure pages from the start of Chapter 1 to the end of the final chapter and so they include tables and figures but do *not* include the table of contents, the list of references or the appendices. Note that some months have been added to direct percentage durations for the first and final chapters, to allow for the start and the final drafting of the thesis. I have assumed that the margins, the font and the line spacing are those described below (that is, 3 cm left margin and 2.54 cm other margins, 12 point Times New Roman font and 1.5 line spacing).

Table 2 — An approximate plan for a 65 000 or so word PhD thesis with two methodologies, completed in 27 months

CHAPTER	TOPIC	%	PAGES	MONTHS
1	Introduction	6	14	2
2	Lit review	33	68	7
3	Methodology I	11	23	3
4	Methodology II	17	37	5
5	Data analysis of methodology II	20	41	5
6	Conclusions	13	27	5
Total		100	210	27

Table 3 — An approximate plan for a 50 000 or so word DBA thesis, completed in 24 months

CHAPTER	TOPIC	%	PAGES	MONTHS
1	Introduction	6	10	3
2	Lit review	34	55	6
3	Methodology	18	30	4
4	Data analysis	22	35	5
5	Conclusions	20	30	6
Total		100	160	24

Table 4 — An approximate plan for a 50 000 or so word DBA thesis with two methodologies, completed in 27 months

CHAPTER	TOPIC	%	PAGES	MONTHS
1	Introduction	6	10	2
2	Lit review	33	52	7
3	Methodology I	11	17	3
4	Methodology II	17	28	5
5	Data analysis of methodology II	20	31	5
6	Conclusions	13	21	5
Total		100	160	27

Links between chapters. With the overall structure justified above, we can turn to how the chapters are linked. Each chapter described below should stand almost alone. Each chapter (except the first) should have an introductory section *linking* the chapter to the main idea of the previous chapter and outlining the *aim* and the *organisation* of the chapter. For example, the core ideas in an introduction to Chapter 3 might be:

> Chapter 2 identified several research issues; this next chapter describes the methodology used to provide data to investigate them. An introduction to the methodology was provided in Section 1.4 of Chapter 1; this chapter aims to build on that introduction and to provide assurance that appropriate procedures were followed. The chapter is organised around four major topics: the study region, the sampling procedure, nominal group technique procedures, and data processing.

The introductory section of Chapter 5 will be longer than those of other chapters, for it will summarise *all* the earlier chapters of the thesis before making conclusions about the research described in those earlier parts; that is, the introduction will repeat the research problem and the research issues/propositions/hypotheses. Each chapter should have a concluding summary section that outlines major themes established in the chapter, *without introducing new material.*

2.2 STYLE USED THROUGHOUT THE THESIS

As well as the structure discussed above, examiners also assess matters of style. Each country and many organisations often have their own style manual. However, three styles are used in many universities around the world: American Psychological Association (APA), *Chicago Manual of Style* (CMS) and Modern Language Association (MLA). The APA style is often used in management, marketing and related theses and is introduced in Faigley (2012), Hacker (2009) and 'Basics of APA Style Tutorial' (2012). These styles cover citations and references but also cover other style issues like commas in a list, a capital after a colon, and a full stop after a contraction.

As an alternative to the three styles above, some Australian candidates could use the spelling, styles and formats of the *Style Manual for Authors, Editors and Printers* (2002) and of the *Macquarie Dictionary*, and so use a consistent style from the first draft and throughout the thesis for processes in their country such as how to emphasise with bold and italics rather than underlining, indent block quotations, use single and double inverted quotation marks, have spaces before and after headings, tables and figures, and gender conventions. After all, the *Style Manual* could be the standard for their later submissions to Australian research funding bodies and to most journals published in Australia. Moreover, using the *Style Manual* or some other manual provides a defensive shield against an examiner from another part of the world who may criticise the thesis from the viewpoint of their own idiosyncratic style. For a start, consider these rules of thumb about style from *Style Manual* (2002, pp. 138, 41):

- Have at least one section or sub-section *heading* per page.
- Have about two to four *paragraphs* under each heading, that is, start at least about three paragraphs per page.
- Have about three to five *sentences* in each paragraph. That is, *do not use one-sentence paragraphs*. Each paragraph should cover one core idea, and that idea should be big enough to warrant more than one sentence, and that idea is summarized in the brief theme or topic sentence that begins the paragraph.

To show thesis examiners that style has been considered as well as formats for citing and referencing, and so they do not need to offer idiosyncratic comments about it, we insert a paragraph like this one at the end of Section 1.5 of a thesis. This sort of paragraph is not needed in a journal article because all the reviewers and the authors are aware of and abide by the style required by that journal:

> This thesis follows styles suggested in Australia's *Style Manual for Authors, Editors and Printers* (2002). Citing and referencing follows that publication, too [or follows the Endnote default bibliographic standard if Endnote cannot be made to incorporate *Style Manual*, as sometimes happens]. Note that when a paragraph has several sentences that obviously have the same source, this thesis adopts the standard procedure of citing the source only once, such as immediately after a specifically named concept or at the end of the first sentence that needs the citation (Marilyn Stone [Technical Editor, the American Marketing Association that publishes A* journals like *Journal of Marketing*] 2011, pers. comm. with Chad Perry, 29 January). The five-chapter structure of this thesis and the terms 'parent theory' and 'research problem theory' in Chapter 2 follow Perry (2002a). Also, this thesis uses spelling checks with the 'English (Australia)' dictionary of Microsoft Word 2007.

In addition to usual style rules such as each paragraph having an early theme or topic sentence, a thesis has some style rules of its own. For example, Chapter 1 is usually written in the *present* tense with references to literature in the *past* tense; most of the rest of the thesis is written in the past tense because it concerns the research after it has been done. In more detail, in Chapters 2 and 3, schools of thought and procedural steps are written about using the present tense; but published work and the candidate's own actions are written about using the past tense. For example: 'The eclectic school has [present tense] several strands. Smith (1990) reported [past] that... The first step in content analysis is [present] to decide on categories. The researcher selected [past] ten documents.' In Chapter 4, use the *present* tense for comments about results currently in front of the reader ('The in-depth interviews were [past] more effective, as Table 4.2 shows [present]...'); and for conclusions that are more general than the *specific* results ("In brief, high power distance people are [present] more brutal when...')' (Bem 2002). Finally, in Chapter 5, use the present tense when fitting the conclusions into the body of knowledge, for example, 'This effect is [present] a contribution...' (but use the past tense when referring to the findings from Chapter 4, of course).

In addition, maintain a cool, precise, academic *tone*. Value judgements should not be used in the objective pursuit of truth that a thesis reports. For example, 'it is unfortunate', 'it is interesting', 'it is believed', and 'it is welcome' are inappropriate—they are unjustified value judgements and so are too subjective. For the same reason, the number of adjectives and adverbs should be kept to bare minimum to avoid the impression of being imprecise and flowery. Many adjectives and adverbs lower the academic tone of a thesis or article because they often reflect subjective judgements that are not justified in the sentence. After all, you are not writing propaganda for a rock band! Although first person words such as 'I' and 'my' are now acceptable in a thesis (Bem 2002) (especially in Chapter 3 of a thesis within an interpretive paradigm), the use of the first person should be controlled—the candidate is a mere private in an army pursuing truth and so should not overrate their importance until their degree has been finally awarded. In other words, the candidate should always *justify* any decisions where their judgement was required (such as the number and type of industries surveyed, and the number of points on a Likert scale), acknowledging the strengths and weaknesses of the options considered, and always relying upon as many references as possible to support the decision made.

That is, authorities or evidence should be used to back up any claim of the researcher, if possible. If the examiner wanted to read *opinions*, they could read letters to the editor of a newspaper. Moreover, be polite to others. Few if any authorities in the field should be called 'wrong', at the worst they might be called 'misleading'; after all, one of these authorities might be an examiner and have spent a decade or more developing their positions and so frontal attacks on those positions are likely to be easily repulsed. Indeed, the candidate should try to agree with the supervisor about a panel of possible **examiners** from which the university will select the final thesis examiners, so that only appropriate people are chosen. After all, a greengrocer should not examine meat products, and an academic with a strong positivist background is unlikely to be an appropriate examiner of a qualitative thesis (Easterby-Smith et al. 2008). That is, do not get involved in the crossfire of 'religious wars' of some disciplines. (Above, I refer to a *'panel* of possible examiners' because examiners are usually allowed to say whether their name can be divulged with their report, and if a candidate knows the name of their actual examiners beforehand, then examiners' privacy will not be possible. So a candidate should not know *exactly* who will be their examiners.)

In addition, this early and open consideration of examiners allows the candidate to think about how their ideas will be perceived by likely individual examiners and so express their ideas in a satisfactory way, for example, explain a line of argument more fully or justify a position more completely for an examiner who may not have a strong background in a particular area. One starting point for thinking about who could be an examiner is to consider the journals in which articles about the research may be published during or after the candidature. Then finding out who is the editor and who is on the editorial board of these journals will be a starting point for thinking about examiners and their interests, publications and styles. That is, a candidate's thesis must communicate with real-life people in an easily-followed way. By the way, most universities allow a candidate to say who should not be among the examiners; and the candidate should ensure their supervisor does not select an examiner who has not supervised a PhD to completion and who has not previously examined a PhD thesis—this type of PhD examiner is almost always a hopeless examiner (Mullins & Kiley 2002).

This issue of communication with examiners is crucial. Consider an examiner. They may be reading the thesis at 11 pm on Friday after a hard day's work on more important things like their own research, their own candidates' PhD research or morale in their Department; most examiners cannot find the time during work hours to read a thesis (Mullins & Kiley 2002). (Thus a major reason for their agreeing to examine the thesis is a sense of duty to their discipline.) So the candidate should try to make the process of examination as much like a journey on 'autopilot' as possible, with the track clearly flagged, changes in direction clearly marked, and each step in an argument explicitly explained, as described below. In other words, the reader must be guided along a smooth, easily-followed path towards the conclusions that have excited the candidate and will hopefully excite the examiner into passing the thesis, and even perhaps asking the candidate to work with the examiner on a research project in the future.

This easily-followed communication can be achieved by using five principles. Firstly, have sections and sub-sections starting as often as every second or third page, each with a descriptive heading in bold. Secondly, start each section or sub-section with a phrase or sentence linking it with what has gone before, for example, a sentence might start with 'Given the situation described in Section 2.3.4' or 'Turning from international issues to domestic concerns, ...' The important point here is that the examiner is led on from old ideas that they have already digested, to new ideas; we all need 'an opportunity to get "comfortable" with old material before new material is thrown at us' (Lindsay 1995, p. 56). Thirdly, briefly describe the argument or point to be made in the section or paragraph in a theme/topic sentence at its beginning, for example, 'Seven deficiencies in models in the literature will be identified'. The next principle of easily-followed communication is to make each step in an argument easy to identify with or the judicious use of linkers such as 'firstly', 'secondly', or 'moreover', 'in addition', 'in contrast' and so on. (Handy lists of such linkers are at 'The writer's handbook using transitions' 2012) Finally, end each section with a summary, to establish what it has achieved; this summary sentence or paragraph could be flagged by usually beginning it with 'In conclusion, ...' or 'In brief, ...' Maintaining these five principles will make arguments easy to follow and so guide the examiner towards agreeing with a candidate's views.

There are other style rules. One rule is that the word 'etc.' is too imprecise to be used in a thesis. Furthermore, words such as 'this', 'these', 'those' and 'it' should not be left *dangling*—they should always refer to an object; for example, 'This rule should be followed' is preferred to 'This should be followed'. Some supervisors also suggest that brackets should be rarely used in a thesis—if a comment is important enough to help answer the thesis' research problem, then it should be added in a straightforward way and not be hidden within brackets as a minor concern to distract the examiner away from the research problem.

As well, definite and indefinite articles should be avoided where possible, especially in headings; for example, the heading 'Supervision of doctoral candidates' is tauter and less presumptuous than 'The supervision of doctoral candidates'. Paragraphs should be short; as a rule of thumb, three to four paragraphs should start on each page if my preferred line spacing of 1.5 and Times New Roman 12 point serif font is used, so as to provide adequate structure and complexity of thought on each page. Rarely use italics or bold for emphasis—a rule of thumb seems to be to limit such emphases in a thesis to three or less words per page (yes, there are more than this number on many pages in this book chapter but this is not a thesis or an article). A final note of style is that most margins should be those nominated by the university or the standard below of 3 cms for the left margin and 2.54 for the other margins.

Final considerations. The above comments about structure and style correctly imply that a thesis with its readership of one, two or three knowledgeable examiners is different from a book that has a very wide readership among relatively ignorant undergraduate candidates (Derricourt 1992), and is different from shorter conference papers and journal articles which do not require the burden of proof and references to broader bodies of knowledge required in theses. Candidates should be aware of these differences and could therefore consider concentrating on completing the thesis before adapting parts of it for conferences and journals. However presenting a paper at a conference during a candidature may lead to useful contacts with the 'invisible college' of researchers in a field (Rogers 1983, p. 57). As well, some candidates have found reviewers' comments on conference papers and articles submitted during their candidacy have improved the quality of their thesis' analysis (and publication has helped them get a job). Moreover, writing an article or conference paper may help to overcome a thesis writer's 'writer's block'.

The thesis will have to go through many drafts that show a progression from the creative, right side of the brain to the more logical, left side of the brain (Zuber-Skerritt & Knight 1986). The first draft will be started early in the candidature, after the establishment of a tentative table of contents of each chapter and their sections along the lines of Table 1. This first draft works on the right, creative side of the brain and emphasises basic ideas without much concern for detail or precise language that come in later drafts. After the first rough draft, later drafts will be increasingly crafted through the left, analytical side of the brain and emphasise fine tuning of arguments, justification of positions and further evidence gathering from other research literature. Supervisors and other candidates should be involved in the review of these drafts because research has shown that good researchers 'require the collaboration of others to make their projects work, to get them to completion' (Frost & Stablein 1992, p. 253), and that social isolation is the main reason for withdrawing from postgraduate study (Phillips & Conrad 1992). By the way, research has also shown that relying on just one supervisor can be dangerous (Conrad, Perry & Zuber-Skerritt 1992; Phillips & Conrad 1992).

2.3 CHUNKINESS IN A THESIS

The concept of a 'chunk' can help summarise some of the discussion above. As shown at the start of the thesis in Section 1.2, the whole thesis is one big chunk of an idea. But each part of the thesis should be a chunky part of the whole thesis, with links to other parts. For a start, each *chapter* should have its own role within the thesis such as Chapter 2's identification of research issues about which data is collected in Chapter 3. Each chapter has *section* and *subsection* chunks with a numbering system that reflects their interrelationships (such as 3.2, 3.2.1 and 3.2.2). Then each subsection has chunks of paragraphs within it, sometimes indicated with run-in headings.

Next there are individual *paragraphs*. These are almost always longer than just one sentence and take up about one third of a page or so. Each paragraph usually has a 'linker' word at the start such as 'Next' or 'Furthermore'. These linkers at the start of a paragraph lead the examiner from already-digested ideas into a new idea. Each paragraph deals with one idea that is introduced and summarised in a theme/topic sentence near the start, for the start of a paragraph is a 'hot spot' that the reader will normally concentrate upon (Lindsay 1995). Finally, each sentence has one small idea, with the most important aspect of the sentence presented at its start; that is, do not waste the hot spot at the start of a sentence on a relatively unimportant phrase like 'As shown in Table 6', rather, place these unimportant phrases at the end of a sentence after a comma. Sentences also often have a linker word at the start such as 'However' to guide the reader from the known content of the previous sentence into the new material in the sentence. If there is no linker, the reader will assume the new sentence leads directly from the previous sentence. In brief, the thesis should be a string of clear chunks of ideas.

The example below will illustrate this easily-followed chunkiness. Notice in the example:

- the *hierarchy of paragraphs* from a side heading with a number, through a side heading without a number, to a run-on heading that leads into two or three paragraphs of text
- the *headings* are descriptive, rather than terse one- or two-word announcements (*Style Manual* 2002, p. 139)
- *some text follows each heading*, for example, even though

the second side heading closely follows the first, there is nevertheless some text between the two headings
- *the text reads as though the headings* were not there, that is, the reader can skip the headings and still not miss the argument (Style Manual 2002, p. 139)
- the *text outlines the topics* to be covered in each section before going into the details of those topics.

Here is the example (adapted from McKinsey 1994, pp. 42-43):

3.1 Why some joint initiatives work and others do not.
While there is still much to learn about joint initiatives in Australia, our observations of high-growth firms overseas and of Australia's shipbuilders have provided insights into what works and what barriers are still to be overcome.

Some common features of successful joint initiatives.
There appear to be three necessary ingredients in successful joint initiatives: a large and/or expanding market, and complementary interests and skill. Physical proximity may also be important in joint initiatives other than those with customers, suppliers and R&D providers.

Large and/or expanding market. The most successful joint initiatives among Australia's high-growth firms were often in industries with large or expanding markets—and for Australia that means export markets. A strong export orientation creates a common focus and the sense of a bigger pie that allows partners to work together. This common perspective is often absent when firms compete for a small domestic market. The shipbuilding and downstream chemical industries in Australia and abroad provide two contrasting examples of this. Norwegian shipbuilders....

On the other hand, the domestic focus and history of competition among downstream chemical firms in Australia may help to explain their lack of enthusiasm for joint initiatives compared with their Norwegian counterparts....

Complementary interests and skills.
Complementary interests and skills seem to be important, if obvious, ingredients of successful joint initiatives. It is not enough to simply get together—firms must have enough common ground

to be useful to one another. Hunternet is a good example of how a network of firms with diverse but complementary interests can become a force for innovation and growth....

3 DETAILS OF CHAPTERS AND THEIR SECTIONS

Turning from the general issues of style and structure above to more precise details about a thesis, each chapter of a thesis and its parts are discussed next.

3.1 CHAPTER 1 INTRODUCTION

Chapter 1 sets the scene for the whole thesis and has the following numbered sections.

Section 1.1 Background to the research
Section 1.1 outlines the broad field of study and then leads into the focus of the research problem. This section is short and aims to orient the readers and grasp their attention. Section 1.1 goes from the overall field down to the gap in that literature that the research problem will encapsulate, as shown in the triangle in Figure 2. A thesis should be able to reference at least four or five previous researchers in each of the first one or two paragraphs, to demonstrate from the start of the thesis that care has been taken to acknowledge and chart the depth and breadth of the existing body of knowledge. Most of the material in Section 1.1 is covered in more detail in later sections such as Section 1.3, and so these sections will have to be referred to in Section 1.1; indeed, Section 1.1 is usually only about one or two pages maximum. For this reason, Section 1.1 is often one of the last sections of Chapters 1 and 2 to be written.

Figure 2 — The triangle of Section 1.1 of Chapter 1

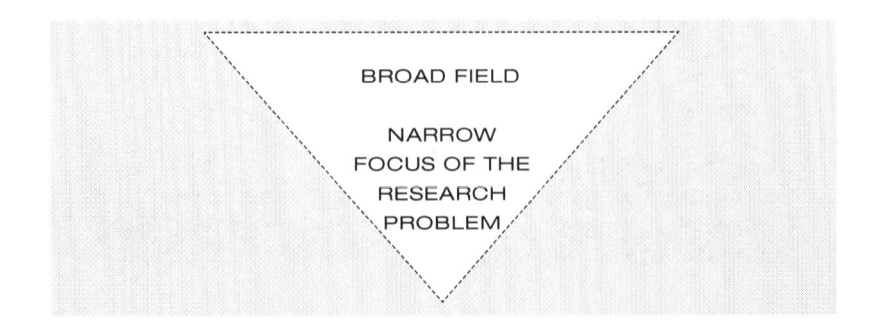

BROAD FIELD

NARROW FOCUS OF THE RESEARCH PROBLEM

Section 1.1 could use either a 'field of study' approach or an 'historical review' approach. For example, using a field of study approach, Section 1.1 of a thesis about a firm's licensing of technology would start with comments about international trade and development, Australia's GDP, the role of new product and process development in national economic growth, and then have an explanation of how technology licensing helps a firm's new product and new process development, leading into a sentence about how little research has been done into it.

An alternative to the field of study example of the previous paragraph is to provide a brief historical review of ideas in the field, leading up to the present. If this alternative approach to structuring Section 1.1 is adopted, it cannot replace the comprehensive review of the literature to be made in Chapter 2, and so numerous references will have to be made to Chapter 2. While the brief introductory history review may be appropriate for a journal article, Section 1.1 of a thesis should usually take the field of study approach illustrated in the paragraph above, to prevent repetition of its points in Chapter 2.

Section 1.2 Research problem, research issues propositions/hypotheses and contributions

Section 1.2 covers core parts of the research report. To begin, it outlines the one big idea of the research, starting with the *research problem* printed in bold or italics on page 1 or 2 of the thesis. The research problem is often one or two sentences that cannot be answered 'yes' or 'no'; it is the broad problem that the researcher will examine more precisely later in the research issues/propositions/hypotheses, and is the problem prompting and placing a boundary around the research without specifying what kind of research is to be done (Emory & Cooper 1991). 'The statement of the research problem *must* imply that, for the resolution of the problem, *thinking on the part of the researcher* will be required' (Leedy 1989, p. 61). Sometimes there may be sub-problems to the major research problem.

Examples of a research problem in a Master's thesis are:

- How and why do New South Wales and Queensland private sector managers successfully implement telemarketing into their organisations?
- How and why do Australian manufacturers select distribution channels for their exports to Japan?

The research problem in a PhD thesis is often more theoretical than these two examples from Master's theses above, for a PhD research problem should not be merely a 'problem-solving' one but should be 'testing-out' the limits of previously proposed generalisations (Phillips & Pugh 2000, p. 50). That is, '[PhD] research, even when narrowly and tightly defined, should be guided by some explicit theoretical or conceptual framework' and without this framework, the thesis becomes a 'mindless ... theoretical wasteland' (Adams & White 1994, pp. 566, 574). That conceptual framework will be developed in Chapter 2, but one or two of its constructs would be reflected in the research problem. Examples of appropriate PhD research problems are:

- How culturally appropriate is TQM for 'reconceptualising' African management?
- How effective for strategic marketing in the Australian finance industry are Porter's models of competition and European models of networks?

Note that the constructs referred to in the research problem are high level ones and are not the more specific constructs developed for testing as research issues/ propositions/hypotheses at the end of Chapter 2, or their operational definitions developed in Chapter 3.

When formulating the research problem, its boundaries or delimitations should be carefully considered, even if these considerations are not made explicit in the wording of the research problem. It requires judgement to decide how 'delimited' the statement of a research problem should be. Examiners are academics and they want academic research to be different from the research done by mere consultants that is very context-specific, for example, developed for just one firm. Thus, the research problem in a PhD thesis about the finance industry in Australia might be advised to not include 'Australia' in the research problem statement. The thesis might then simply refer to 'Australia' in a sentence after the research problem statement, or even leave mention of it to the delimitations in Section 1.7. This 'judgment call' about how context-specific the research problem statement should be, probably depends on the importance of the context to the contributions of the thesis. For example, if Australia was merely a research setting in a PhD thesis and was not expected to affect results much, then Australia could be left out of the research problem statement. However, if a DBA thesis' contributions were based upon its Malaysian context, then 'Malaysia' should be included in the research problem statement. This issue of the context of research is explored further in the discussion of Chapter 2 below.

In effect, the research problem and the delimitations in the later Section 1.7 outline the research area, setting explicit or implicit boundaries for its applicability to:

- one broad area of interest, for example, 'telecommunications marketing', (candidates might consider ensuring that this one area of interest has its *own* academic discipline from which several examiners could be selected—a two-discipline thesis requiring examiners from two different disciplines may produce conflicts among examiners)
- level of decision making, for example, directors, managing directors, senior managers, customers, or public policy analysts
- private or public sector organisation
- industry, for example, transport industry
- geographic limits, for example, Queensland or Australia
- time or business cycle limits, for example, in the late 1980s before the Australian economy entered a recession.

Asking the familiar questions of 'who', 'what', 'where', 'how' and 'why' (Yin 2009, p. 27) may lead the candidate towards placing these appropriate boundaries around the research problem.

All the boundaries of the research problem will be explicit in the research problem or in Section 1.7; however, *all* the boundaries should be *justified* in Section 1.7. In the example above, restricting the research problem to Queensland and New South Wales' telemarketing could be based on those states being more advanced than the rest of Australia. That is, the boundaries cannot be arbitrary. Within those boundaries, the data and the conclusions of this PhD research should apply; outside those boundaries, it can be questioned whether the results will apply.

Thus identifying the research problem will take some time, and is an exercise in a 'progressive reduction of uncertainty' while it is narrowed and refined to cover a gap in the literature (Phillips & Pugh 2000, p. 86). Nevertheless, early identification of a preliminary research problem focuses research activity and literature searches, and so is an important early part of the research project (Zuber-Skerritt & Knight 1986). An example of the gradual narrowing of a research problem is a candidate's problem about the partners in a small Australian architectural practice that initially referred to 'practice of strategic management', then to 'designing and implementing a strategy', then to 'implementing a strategy', and then finally to 'the processes involved in implementing a strategy'.

After the research problem is presented, a short paragraph should say how the problem will be solved in the thesis. This step is necessary because academic writing should not be a detective story with the solution kept a mystery until the end (Brown 1995). An example of this paragraph following a research problem statement is:

> The problem addressed in this research is: *How can relationships involved in inter-organisational governance in marketing channels be managed?* Essentially, I argue that inter-organisational governance is a heterogeneous phenomenon and that different relationship management strategies are appropriate under different conditions. (based on Heide 1994, p. 71)

Another example of a research problem and its solution in Section 1.2 is:

> The problem addressed in this research is: *Which of the three major paradigms best explains strategic decision making?* I conclude that strategic decision makers are boundedly rational, that power wins battles of choice and chance matters. I also propose a new agenda for future research which centres on a few, key research areas and opens up research to new paradigms. (based on Eisenhardt & Zbaracki 1992, pp. 17-18)

This openness right at the beginning of a thesis about the positions that will be developed later should also be shown in chapters, sections and even in paragraphs. That is, *expectations are created* about the intellectual positions that will be developed later in the chapter, section and paragraph (in the topic sentence of a paragraph), then those expectations are *fulfilled* and finally a conclusion *confirms* those expectations have been met.

After the research problem and a brief summary of how it will be solved is presented in Section 1.2, the section presents the major bodies of theory that will be covered in Chapter 2 (in about one page or so) and then lists the *research issues/propositions/hypotheses* that will be developed in Chapter 2 to focus later data collection and analysis. The research problem above usually refers to decisions; in contrast, the research issues/propositions/ hypotheses usually require *information* for their solution. The research issues or propositions/hypotheses are the specific questions that the researcher will gather data about in order to satisfactorily solve the research problem (Emory & Cooper 1991). The research issues or propositions/ hypotheses listed after the research problem in Section 1.2 are developed in Chapter 2, so they are little more than merely listed in Section 1.2. The section states that they are established in Chapter 2 and notes the sections in which they appear in that chapter.

Note that early drafts of parts of Chapters 1 and 2 are written *together* from the start of the candidature, although not necessarily in the order of their sections (Nightingale 1992). That is, the major ideas in Chapters 1 and 2 should have been crystallised in drafts before the research work described in Chapter 3 starts, and the thesis is not left to be 'written up' after the research. It is especially important that Chapter 2 is crystallised *before* the data collection actually starts, to prevent the data collection phase missing important data or wasting time on unimportant material. In other words, the research 'load' must be identified, sorted out and tied down before the 'wagon' of research methodology begins to roll. Despite this precaution, candidates will probably have to continue to rewrite some parts of Chapters 1 and 2 towards the end of their candidature, while their understanding of the research area continues to develop.

As part of the approach to a thesis not being a detective story, that was noted above, this Section 1.2 should then briefly describe the *contributions* that the thesis will make in its final chapter. This description should be limited to less than one or two pages. This part could begin with: 'Answering the research issues provided contributions that will be presented in Section 5.2. In summary, this research made seven contributions. Firstly, ...'

That is, the solution to the research problem should make a contribution to the literature. Exactly what is a contribution can be somewhat controversial (Phillips 1992). Making a doctorate's distinct contribution to knowledge is merely 'normal' research (rather than paradigm-busting research) (Phillips and Pugh 2000, p. 36)—it should not aim to win a Nobel Prize (Mullins & Kiley 2002). One way of checking whether the solution to a proposed research problem will make a contribution is to use a library database like ABI/INFORM or EBSCOHost to search for articles that have keywords that are the parent theories from Chapter 2 (by using the Boolean operator AND). If there is no such article or there is only one or two of them, the thesis about that research problem will probably make a contribution. So making a contribution about the intersection of the parent theories should not be too difficult if the thesis' chapters have been carefully designed and executed as explained here.

Bringing two parent theories together for the first time is not the only way of making a contribution. That is, PhD research need 'not go beyond the goal of stretching the body of knowledge slightly' and so could use a relatively new methodology in a field, use a methodology in a country where it has not been used before, or make a synthesis or interpretation that has not been made before (Phillips and Pugh 2000, p. 35; Philips 1992; Murray 2002). For an example of this way of making a contribution, consider how a doctoral candidate's Section 1.2 carefully and explicitly made the case that he had made a contribution by applying an *existing theory* in a *new setting* of an industry where it had not been applied before:

> This research about how to market the services of funeral homes in Australia is justified for two reasons: it addresses an under-researched area and its focus is the sizable Australian funeral market. That is, it fulfils the criterion for a contribution in a doctoral thesis confirmed by the authoritative guide of Phillips and Pugh (2000, p. 35), *How to Get a PhD:* a contribution is applying an established theory in a new setting. In this thesis, the established theory is 'strategic management processes' and the new setting is the 'Australian funeral industry'. Similarly, Philips (1992, p. 128) notes about an original contribution, after a survey of staff at the University of New South Wales:
>
> > *it was not necessary to have a whole new way of looking at things... people could be original in a number of ways... trying out something in this country that has previously only been done in other countries.*
>
> This section and the literature review in Chapter 2 about the established theory and about the unusual industry where the theory had not been applied before, justifies that this thesis makes a contribution. (based on Morelli 2010, p. 1-2)

Of course, the new setting must be suitably different from the settings of previous research—there must be explicit consideration of why the new setting *could* produce different results; the new setting could be in a new industry or a new culture, for instance. For example, replicating US research about mobile phones in another country would not make a sufficient contribution unless cultural or regulatory differences in the new country could logically provide different results, and this difference had been patiently explained in Section 1.2 and Chapter 2 of the thesis. If a new setting is the basis for a thesis' contribution, the *setting* should be described in Chapter 2.

Section 1.3 Justification for the research
Examiners are concerned that the candidate has addressed an important research area and not a trivial one. It is not enough to show there are gaps in the body of knowledge; they must be *important gaps* (Varadarajan 1966). That is, the research problem should be important on several theoretical and practical grounds; for example, a thesis could justify its research problem through these four points, starting with the theory gap or contribution because that is the gap that most interests an examiner before moving on to other demonstrations that the gap is an important one:

i   The research outcomes will be innovative and novel by describing the relative neglect of the specific research problem by previous researchers (some of this justification in Section 1.3 would refer to Chapter 2, for there is no need to repeat parts of Chapter 2 here; however, Chapter 2 deals mainly with the nitty-gritty of individual research issues while this Section 1.3 should emphasise the *whole* research problem and possibly conclude with some appropriate quotes from authorities about the research problem). That is, this Section 1.3 describes how the anticipated outcomes of the research will advance the knowledge base of the discipline.

ii The importance and complexity of the industry and/or the importance of the specific area being investigated like parts of a supply chain or of a management process. This justification is usually accompanied by a mass of statistical data showing how huge the area of the research problem is in terms of constructs such as revenue, employment and assets, and is sometimes accompanied by authoritative discussions and quotations from government publications about committees of inquiry, to show how the research might result in national economic, environment and/or social benefits.

iii The relative neglect of the research's methodologies by previous researchers in the thesis' field (with references to Chapter 3 being required here, with an acknowledgment that the methodology is *justified* there and is not simply used for the sake of novelty).

iv The usefulness of *future, potential* applications of the research's findings to organisations and other relevant end-users (this justification is based on the researcher's initial assumptions *at the start of the research project*; in contrast, the implications in Section 5.4 are about the completed research's usefulness).

Section 1.4 Methodology
Section 1.4 is an introductory overview of the methodology, and is placed here in Chapter 1 to satisfy the initial curiosity of the examiner. This section should refer to sections in Chapters 2 and 3 where the methodology is described and justified in far more detail. Because of the openness of thesis writing noted above, this section introduces the data analysis methods as well as the data collection methods, and briefly summarises the findings of the data analysis.

That is, this section first describes the methodology in general terms, including a brief, one- or two- paragraph description of major statistical processes, for example, of regression. Then the section could refer to sections in Chapter 2 where methodology is discussed. Section 1.4 could possibly justify the chosen methodology based upon the purpose of the research, and justify not using other techniques. For example, the choice of a mail survey rather than a telephone survey or case studies could be briefly justified. Alternatively and preferably, this justification for the methodology used could be left until the review of previous research in Chapter 2 and the start of Chapter 3. Details of the methodology such as the sampling frame and the size of the sample are provided in Chapter 3 and not in Section 1.4.

In summary, this section merely helps to provide an overview of the research methodology, and can be perfunctory—two pages would be a maximum length.

Section 1.5 Outline of this report
Each chapter of the thesis/report is briefly described in this section. (Incidentally, the candidate must use either 'report' or 'thesis' consistently.)

Section 1.6 Definitions
Definitions adopted by researchers are often not uniform, so key and controversial terms are defined to establish positions taken in the academic research. (The previous sentence could be used to begin this section). The term being defined should be in italics or in bold, and the format for presenting each of the definitions should be standard. Definitions should match the underlying assumptions of the research and candidates may need to justify most of their definitions. The definitions will underlie the

data collection procedures and so put boundaries around the findings (although literature using other definitions will of course be included in the literature reviewed in Chapter 2). A definition of a core construct may be discussed in depth later at the beginning of Chapter 2, and defining the construct in this Section 1.6 can merely present the definition and refer to the discussion in Chapter 2.

Candidates should try to use definitions that have been adopted by authorities wherever possible, so that the results of the research can be fitted into the body of literature and so that the thesis can withstand attacks by examiners with trivial personal preferences. For example, a recent statistics textbook or article could be used as a standard for research procedures and terms (but their definitions of terms such as 'construct', 'research issue', 'hypothesis' and 'operational definition' are assumed for the thesis). Perhaps the candidate could make some minor changes to a standard definition to make it particularly appropriate to the thesis; doing this will illustrate a critical mind at work which is aware of the overriding need to solve the research problem. Justification for some of these definitions might have to refer to the next section about the justified delimitations of the thesis, but do not use definitions that restrict the generalisability of the findings too much.

Section 1.7 Delimitations of scope and key assumptions, with their justifications
This delimitations section 'builds a fence' around the research findings that are additional to the limitations and key assumptions established in the previous section about definitions. For example, the explicit boundaries of the research problem described in Section 1.2 above should be noted again in this section and other boundaries should be clearly expressed. Other delimitations could be the industries chosen, the locations chosen, environmental factors, and variables that could not be controlled. In effect, the 'population' about which findings are to be made, is outlined here.

In this Section 1.7, the researcher is trying to forestall examiners' criticisms, so *justifications* for these delimitations must be provided. It would be wise to not mention that time and/or resources were major influences on these delimitations of the research, because an examiner may think that the candidate should have chosen a research project that was more appropriate for these obvious delimitations of any research. So, the candidate always has to think of other justification for a delimitation, for example, the different cultural and/or economic contexts that exist beyond the delimited boundary. No claims for the *conclusions* beyond these delimitations will be made, although *implications* of the findings beyond the delimitations may be made.

Incidentally, 'delimitations' are sometimes called 'limitations' in some theses and is common in US theses. Strictly speaking, by definition, 'delimitations' are within the control of the researcher and 'limitations' are not. The term of delimitation refers to the planned, justified *scope* of the study beyond which generalisation of the results was not intended. For example, a limitation may be that a very good sampling frame could not be found, and a delimitation may be that the research was restricted to financial services industries because of their special nature that was appropriate to the research. In turn, in most theses, the limitations caused specifically by the methodological methods chosen are not here in Section 1.7 but are placed in a section of Chapter 3 or in Section 5.6 along with any other limitations. Some candidates might like to describe the unit of analysis here in Section 1.7, for example, firm or manager. Whether it is described here or in Chapter 3 where it should be, is not important—just as long as it is identified and justified somewhere in the thesis.

Section 1.8 Conclusion
The final paragraph of each thesis chapter usually summarises the key achievements of the chapter. So the conclusion of Chapter 1 should read something like:

> This chapter laid the foundations for the report. It introduced the research problem and research issues. Then the research was justified, definitions were presented, the methodology was briefly described and justified, the report was outlined, and the limitations were given. On these foundations, the report can proceed with a detailed description of the research.

3.2 CHAPTER 2 RESEARCH ISSUES

The second thesis chapter aims to build a theoretical foundation upon which the research is based by reviewing the relevant literature to identify research issues that are worth researching because they are controversial and/or have not been answered by previous researchers. That is, the literature review is not an end in itself, but is a means to the end of identifying the worthy research issues that will be listed in the chapter's conclusion and were briefly introduced to the examiner in Section 1.2.

It is this point about the chapter being a means to an end that prompts its title being 'Research issues' rather than 'Literature review'. Incidentally, the chapter is about the extant literature, so the candidates' own ideas or opinions have no place in this chapter, except where they are used to structure the treatment of the literature and to create the conceptual framework at the end of the chapter, and are clearly supported by authorities, evidence or logic.

Chapter 2 covers the research problem theory and parent theories. The survey of the literature in a thesis does concentrate on the area of the research problem described in Section 1.2, for it includes the *research problem theory* of the research problem (for example, employee motivation or customer service). But the literature review should also demonstrate a familiarity with some *parent theories* (for example, employee psychology or services marketing). University of Oregon (n.d.) called these two types of 'theories' the parent and immediate disciplines. In turn, the authorities Phillips and Pugh (2000) descriptively named these two types of theories as background and focus theories, respectively. I prefer to combine these two sources into the 'parent theory' and the 'research problem theory' because 'parent' emphasises that the parent must be relevant to resolving the research problem and not any mere background theory, and 'research problem' emphasises why the research problem theory is a focus of the end of Chapter 2. Figure 3 shows this pattern of parent and research problem theories.

Figure 3 — The link between the research problem and the conceptual framework developed in the research problem theory to solve it, and the parent theories and the research issues or propositions/hypotheses

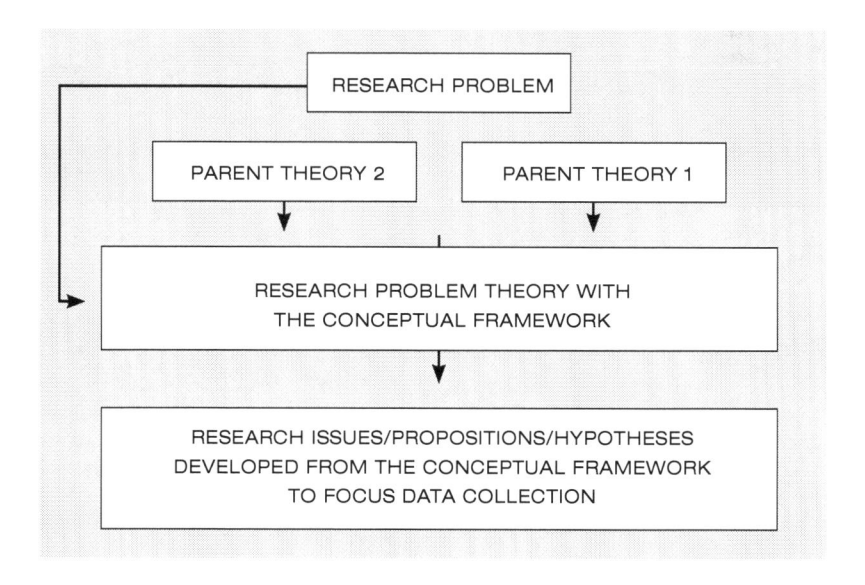

```
                    ┌─────────────────────┐
            ┌───────│  RESEARCH PROBLEM   │
            │       └─────────────────────┘
            │
            │   ┌──────────────────┐   ┌──────────────────┐
            │   │ PARENT THEORY 2  │   │ PARENT THEORY 1  │
            │   └────────┬─────────┘   └────────┬─────────┘
            │            │                      │
            │            ▼                      ▼
            │   ┌──────────────────────────────────────────┐
            └──▶│   RESEARCH PROBLEM THEORY WITH           │
                │   THE CONCEPTUAL FRAMEWORK               │
                └──────────────────┬───────────────────────┘
                                   ▼
                ┌──────────────────────────────────────────┐
                │  RESEARCH ISSUES/PROPOSITIONS/HYPOTHESES │
                │  DEVELOPED FROM THE CONCEPTUAL FRAMEWORK │
                │         TO FOCUS DATA COLLECTION         │
                └──────────────────────────────────────────┘
```

Consider what a *parent theory* is, in more detail. Essentially, it is a body of knowledge like sustainable tourism, events tourism, relationship marketing, organisational learning, Internet marketing, consumer behaviour.... There could be a journal about them; for example, the journal could be the one you would like to publish articles about your thesis in. There could be tracks about them at conferences—get a CD with some conference proceedings to find these. A university could offer a degree subject (or a major part of a subject) about them. In your coverage of each parent theory, start broad and then narrow: define the term, then briefly cover major themes within it, and then explore in depth the theme or sub-theme most relevant for this research. A literature review should contain parent theories that are *directly* relevant to the research problem theory—other indirectly associated theories should be relegated to Section 5.4 of the thesis as areas for which the research has implications. In other words, only direct parent theories needed to develop a conceptual framework in the research problem theory are involved, not *indirect* relatives like grandparent, uncle or aunt theories.

That is, a candidate's research about the research problem theory should be 'testing out' previous research, that is, research which tests out the limits of previously proposed, parent theories (Phillips & Pugh 2000). For example, theory about marketing brands has almost been completely based on research about goods; PhD research could test out whether this goods-based theory applies to services as well as goods. Brands and services marketing would be the parent theories and the research problem theory would consider them together.

Another example would be to test out whether the theory about relationship marketing applies to cyber marketing. Yet another example would be to test whether traditional theory about product strategy applies in database marketing. Thus this concept of testing out research is valuable for ensuring postgraduate research makes a contribution (as discussed in the treatment of Section 1.2 and 1.3 above) and helps the design of Chapter 2.

The relationships between several of the concepts above are shown in Figure 4. In that figure, the literature review covers the parent theories and the research problem theory. Note that the research problem theory is only about the research problem. Of all possible aspects of the research problem, only some aspects are within the delimited scope described in Section 1.7, but the literature reviewed about the research problem theory usually covers *all* aspects of the research problem.

That is, in Figure 3, some boundaries of the research problem are made explicit in Section 1.2 and all are made explicit in Section 1.7; this difference is shown by some but not all of the line around the boundaries of the delimited research problem in the figure being the same as the line around the research problem area. All boundaries of the research problem should have been justified in Section 1.7, as noted above.

Figure 4 — Relationships between the parent theories and research problem theory, and between the research problem and the research issues or propositions/hypotheses

- Literature review, including parent disciplines
- Research problem area (presented in Section 1.2 and justified in Section 1.3)
- Boundaries of research problem, for rexample, Queensland or the public sector (justified in Section 1.7)
- Parts of the research problem studied in previous research (discussed in Chapter 2)
- Research questions or hypotheses not answered in previous research (justified in Chapter 2)

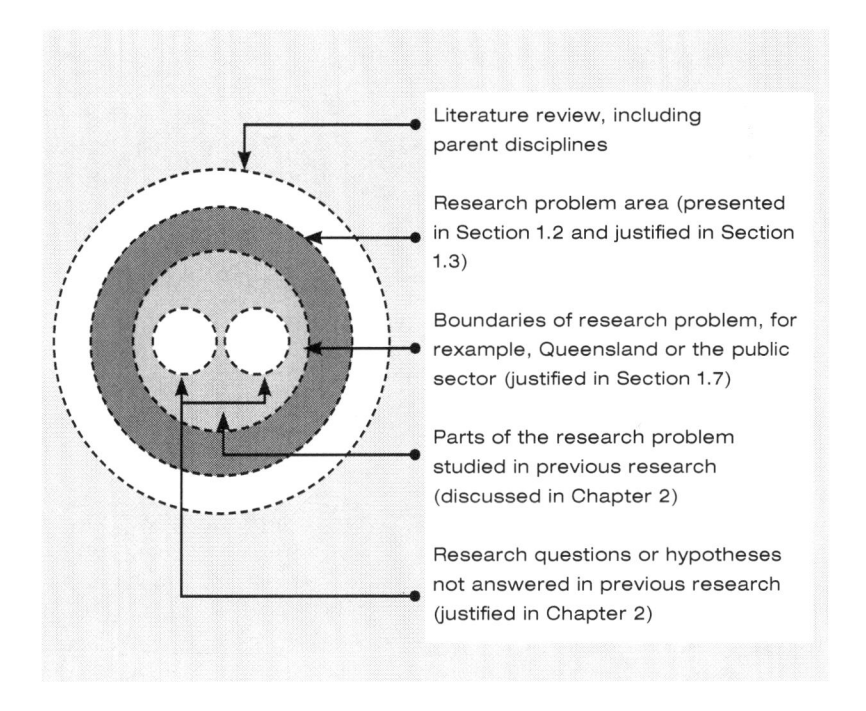

Figure 4 also shows that some of the literature about the research problem theory will already provide some answers to parts of the research problem, but it is the *gaps* of un- or under-researched or controversial parts of the research problem about which the research will collect data. That is, the statements of the research issues or propositions/hypotheses about these gaps are the ultimate goal of Chapter 2, and provide a focus for the data collection and analysis described in the next two chapters.

Classification models of the parent theories and analytical models of the conceptual framework. Some judgment may be required to balance the need to focus on the research problem theory, and the need for a thesis to show familiarity with the literature of the parent theories. Consider the *parent theories* first. In a parent theory, develop 'mind maps' such as a new classification model of the body of knowledge of the parent theory, showing how concepts can be grouped together according to schools of thought or themes, without necessarily considering relationships between the groups (Figure 3 is an example). These concepts could be the section headings in the outline of the chapter that should precede the writing of the chapter (Zuber-Skerritt & Knight 1986). The new classification model will begin to show that the candidate's literature survey is constructively analytical rather than merely descriptive, for the rigor in a thesis should be predominantly at the upper levels of Bloom and Krathowl's (1956) six-level hierarchy of educational objectives. Levels 1, 2 and 3 are mere knowledge, comprehension and application that every undergraduate should display. Levels 4, 5 and 6 are analysis, synthesis and evaluation—the higher-order skills that academic examiners consider a postgraduate research candidate should develop (Easterby-Smith et al. 2008).

Presenting a classification model of the sections of the whole chapter in a figure near the beginning of Chapter 2 will help the examiners follow the sequence of the chapter. Referring briefly to the figure as each new group of concepts is first discussed, will help the examiner follow the intellectual journey of the chapter. In other words, the literature review is *not* a string of pointless, isolated summaries of the writings of others along the lines of Jones said...Smith said...Green said...' Rather, the links between each writer and others must be brought out, and the links between each writer and the research problem should also be clear. What the candidate says about a writer is more important than a mere description of what a writer says (Leedy 1993). This relative importance is helped by using a bracketed reference like '(Leedy 1993)' in the first part of this sentence, rather than leading with the writer's name by saying 'Leedy (1993) says...'. That is, the thesis should *not be an annotated bibliography* like an undergraduate would write (along the lines of 'Smith (2008) said...'); rather, it demonstrates what the thesis writer thinks about the ideas that the authors have written about and how they have incorporated those ideas into their own thinking and arguments. In brief, to demonstrate this thinking, nearly always place an author's name inside brackets (Bem 2002). In other words, the literature review is not a textbook that describes the literature for a reader who knows little about a topic; rather, it is an interesting rearrangement and synthesis of material with which the examiner should already be familiar.

After the classification models of the parent theories are developed, the *research problem theory* is explored to unearth the research issues or propositions/hypotheses; these should appear to 'grow' out of the discussion as gaps in the body of knowledge are discovered. This research problem theory part of the literature review is clearly different from the parent theory parts, for the candidate's *own* views come to the fore now, as they construct a new conceptual framework that has not been developed previously in the literature—this conceptual framework is used to develop the research issues/propositions/hypotheses about the previously unexplored research problem theory, about which data will be collected in later chapters. The parent theories were merely *the points of departure* for the main journey of the research, that is, the development of the new conceptual framework that is the research problem theory—within this theory, research issues/propositions/hypotheses from the conceptual framework will be used to focus data collection. Indeed, some thesis writers prefer to put this research problem theory into a chapter of its own, to clearly demonstrate how it differs from the somewhat less creative literature review of the parent theories.

This conceptual framework will be more analytical than the classification emphasis of the parent theories—it will usually explicitly consider *relationships* between concepts, and so there will be arrows between the groups of concepts (Figure 1 is an example). This framework is an important part of Chapter 2, for it summarises the conceptual framework from which the research issues/propositions/hypotheses flow at the end of the chapter. Showing appropriate section and subsection numbers on these models (like 2.1, 2.2 and so on) will help referencing of them in the body of the report. In other words, a conceptual framework with justified variables and their relationships that provides an anchor for the development of research issues/propositions/hypotheses towards the end of Chapter 2, is essential.

Examples of the theories. In brief, Chapter 2 reviews the parent and research problem theories, with the aim of charting the body of knowledge with a summary model or two, showing where the research problem fits into that body of knowledge and then identifying research issues or propositions/hypotheses. These issues will focus the discussion of later chapters on directions where further research is required to answer the research problem, that is, having sections in Chapter 3 and 4 explicitly related to the research issues/propositions/hypotheses facilitates the 'seamless' characteristic of an effective thesis.

Of course, each candidate will write Chapter 2 differently because it involves so much personal creativity and understanding and so the chapter's structure may end up being different from that suggested in these notes. Nevertheless, an example of Chapter 2 based on the structure might be useful for beginning research candidates. Note how skilfully the candidates have linked their reviews of the parent and research problem theories.

An example of how to structure Chapter 2 is provided in a PhD thesis that had a research problem about inward technology licensing. Chapter 2 began by developing a definition of inward technology licensing, and then reviewing the parent theory of new product development. In a chronological discussion of major researchers, the review showed a familiarity with major conceptual issues in the parent theory of new product development such as: approaches to new product development which are alternatives to inward technology licensing, the importance of new product development, its riskiness, and its stages with their influencing factors. The review acknowledged disagreements between authorities without developing research issues or propositions/hypotheses, and established that inward technology licensing was an interesting part of the parent theory to research, summarised in a table which compared inward technology licensing with some other methods of new product development on three criteria, using a high-medium-low scale. After fifteen pages of reviewing the parent theory, the chapter addressed the research problem theory of inwards technology licensing by reviewing literature in four groups of influencing factors, summarised in a classification model of the conceptual framework being constructed. As sections of the chapter considered each of these groups, researchers were compared with each other and some hypotheses were developed where controversy or methodological weaknesses existed or research 'gaps' in possibly interesting areas were identified. Particular concepts and the hypothesised directions of relationships between them were summarised in a detailed analytical model that grew out of the earlier classification model used to structure the literature review.

Context of the research. Some candidates might think that the context of the research, that is, the research setting, should also be described in Chapter 2's literature review. But should it be in Chapter 2, or in a chapter of its own or in an appendix? For example, should the economy of Thailand be summarised in the literature review if cases were to be collected in that country, or should the financial services industry in Australia be described if a survey was to be done in that industry in that country? In my own opinion, including a description of the context in Chapter 2's literature review is required only if the main *contribution* of the research depends on this context (this issue was introduced in the discussion of the research problem statement in Section 1.2). For example, consider a candidate who is researching how relationship marketing (which was established in the West) is done in Thailand with its different type of economy and different culture (where the topic has not been researched by academics). That candidate *should* present a background to Thailand as one of the parent theories. But in a second example, a candidate who was researching the effect of Internet marketing on relationships in the financial services industries in Australia would *not* need to include a description of the financial services industry in Chapter 2. The reason is that Internet marketing might be done a bit differently in Australia than the way it is the United States, but that difference is not as important to the research's contributions as the difference between Internet and non-Internet marketing. In this second example, the parent theories would be Internet marketing and relationship marketing, and *examples* from financial services in Australia would be used to illustrate the points being made in those parent theories and in the research problem theory of Chapter 2. In contrast to the first excample, in this second example, a brief description of the Australian economy and Internet activity within it could be placed in Chapter 2 just before the research problem theory is presented, or in Chapter 3, or in an appendix.

Details of Chapter 2. Having established the overall processes of Chapter 2, this discussion can now turn to more detailed considerations. Most pieces of literature should be included in a *summary table* which covers all or most of the details below. The accompanying text does not need to be as detailed unless some of the details are particularly relevant, but the text should nevertheless demonstrate that you have read and understood the role that each reference has played in the development of the body of knowledge, that is, the contribution to the body of knowledge that is *relevant* to the research problem—how it compares and contrasts with the positions developed by other researchers.

The details in the summary table should cover all or most of:

- topics covered, including the year, the industry, the country and/or region, and the subjects in the research (for example, managing directors or middle managers)
- survey and statistical methodologies used
- findings
- limitations and problems of the research, for example, was the data collection or its analysis appropriate?

In brief, providing a concise description of the research topics and methodologies underlying findings reached by writers will provide a basis for the candidates' view of the value of their findings to the body of knowledge, will remind the examiner of the research involved, and will help the candidate to carefully chart the boundaries of the body of knowledge. (Incidentally, it is courteous to reference as many publications as possible of likely examiners.)

Useful guides to how contributions to a body of knowledge can be assessed and clustered into groups for classification and analytical models are found in the many articles in each issue of *The Academy of Management Review*, the literature review parts of articles in the initial overview section of major articles in *The Academy of Management Journal* and other prestigious academic journals, and the chairperson's summing up of various papers presented at a conference. For example, Heide (1994) provides an example of a very analytical treatment of two parent theories and one research problem theory.

If a quotation from a writer is being placed in the literature review or elsewhere in the thesis, the quotation should be preceded by a brief description of what the candidate perceives the writer is saying. For example, the indirect description preceding a quotation might be: 'Zuber-Skerritt and Knight (1986, p. 93) list three benefits of having a research problem to guide research activities: …' Such an indirect description or *precis* preceding a quotation demonstrates that the candidate understands the importance of the quotation and that his or her own ideas are in control of the shape of the review of the literature. Moreover, quotations should not be too long, unless they are especially valuable; the candidate is expected to *precis* long slabs of material in the literature, rather than quote them—after all, the candidate is supposed to be writing the thesis and not the other authors being quoted. For this reason, one supervisor insists on candidates keeping quotations to less than 3 words, and I myself frown upon any quotation approaching 20 or 30 words.

By the way, references in Chapter 2 should include some seminal, landmark references to show that the candidate is aware of the development of the research area, but the chapter must also include *recent* writings—having only old references generally indicates a worn-out research problem. Old references that have made suggestions which have not been subsequently researched might be worth detailed discussion, but why have the suggestions not been researched in the past?

Exploratory/theory building/qualitative research and its research issues. Now consider the two possible pathways developed in Chapter 2 that will guide the data collection and analysis to be described in Chapters 3 and 4. These pathways are exploratory or theory building (qualitative), and explanatory or theory testing (quantitative). First, if the research project's pathway is *exploratory/theory building* and uses a qualitative research procedure such as case studies or action research, then the literature review's conceptual framework in Chapter 2 will unearth *research issues* or questions that will be the focus of the data collection described in later chapters and answered in Chapter 4. (Essentially, exploratory research is qualitative and asks 'what are the variables involved?'; in contrast, explanatory research is quantitative and asks 'what are the precise relationships between variables?' Easterby-Smith et al. (2008) distinguish between qualitative and quantitative methodologies in management research in detail.) Qualitative research issues or questions ask about 'what', 'who' and 'where', for example, and so are not answered with a 'yes' or a 'no', but with a description or discussion. For example, a research issue might be stated as: 'How and why are conflicts between owners and managers that are resolved in the board of directors of a big business, resolved in a small professional practice without a board of directors?'

But note that 'pure' exploratory research or induction that does not use research issues developed in Chapter 2 to guide data collection, is *not* appropriate for PhD research because a body of knowledge (the core of a PhD) is not the foundation for that kind of pure exploratory research (Phillips & Pugh 1994; Perry 1998b). Indeed, Phillips and Pugh (2000, pp. 52-53) assert that pure exploratory research is less likely to produce a contribution to knowledge than the testing out research recommended in this chapter. Nevertheless, the 'impure' exploratory research issues suggested from the literature should supplement and not displace an interviewee's own meanings and interpretations during the qualitative research methodologies often used in a thesis. That is, the research issues provide an indication of areas of interest but may not be the only areas discussed during an interview. For example, an interview should begin with trying to discover the interviewee's *own* meanings and subjective understandings, and the research issues should only be raised as probes towards the end of the interview if their topics have not been discussed in the earlier unstructured discussion (Perry 1998b; Patton 2002).

By the way, the word 'how' in an exploratory research issue does not mean that an experiment is required to establish a direct cause and effect link between A and B. In social science research, such links are very hard to establish and so exploratory research searches for causal *tendencies* or generative mechanisms that suggest a causal relationship only in some limited contexts (Perry, Reige & Brown 1998). As well, as noted earlier, the first person form such as 'I' and 'my' may be used in Chapter 3 of exploratory research theses when describing what the researcher actually did; similarly, many quotations from interviewees should be used in Chapter 4 to illustrate findings.

Explanatory/theory testing/quantitative research and its propositions/ hypotheses. On the other hand, if the research project follows the *explanatory/theory testing* pathway, it refers to hypotheses or propositions at the end of Chapter 2, and uses a quantitative research methodology such as regression analysis of survey data. That is, Chapter 2 unearths testable hypotheses/propositions that can be answered with a 'yes' or 'no', or with a precise answer to questions about 'how many' or 'what proportion' (Emory & Cooper 1991). So, while research issues in exploratory/theory building research are open and require words as data to answer, hypotheses/propositions in explanatory/theory testing research are closed and require *numbers* as data to solve. For example, an hypothesis/ proposition was presented as a question that can be answered 'yes' or 'no' through statistical testing of measured constructs: 'Does the number of successful telemarketing calls correlate with the level of specialisation of telemarketing representatives?'

Each construct in such an hypothesis/proposition (for example, 'specialisation of telemarketing representatives') must be capable of being measured; *precisely* how the instruments were designed to measure the constructs is described later in Chapter 3. That is, operational definitions of the constructs developed for propositions/hypotheses are not divulged until Chapter 3; in other words, the statistical form of a hypothesis involving null and alternative hypotheses about means, distributions or correlation coefficients, for example, is not presented until Chapters 3 and 4. In Chapter 3, the direct links between the propositions and the hypotheses should be made explicit in the text and in a table.

In some PhD research, there may be a mix of qualitative research issues and quantitative hypotheses, for a case research methodology can combine both (Yin 2009). Generally speaking, the total number of research issues and/or propositions/hypotheses should not exceed about four or five or so; if there are more, sufficient analysis may not be done on each within the space constraints of a PhD thesis. Whether hypotheses or propositions are used, they should be presented in the way that informed judges accept as being most likely. For example, the hypothesis/ proposition that 'smoking causes cancer' is preferred to 'smoking does not cause cancer'.

The research issues or propositions/hypotheses developed during Chapter 2 should appear to 'grow out' of the literature review, even though the candidate may have decided on them long before while writing very early drafts of the chapter. That is, the development of the research issues or propositions/hypotheses should make it clear that ideas from the parent theories have laid the groundwork for their development by referring to relevant ideas and gaps in the literatures, and make it clear that they are gaps that this research will fill. And when first presented in Chapter 2, the research issues or propositions/hypotheses should be numbered and indented in bold or italics. The concluding section of Chapter 2 should have a summary list of the research issues or propositions/hypotheses developed earlier in the chapter.

In brief, Chapter 2 identifies and reviews the conceptual/theoretical dimensions of the literature and discovers research issues or propositions/hypotheses from a new conceptual framework that are worth researching in later chapters.

3.3 CHAPTER 3 METHODOLOGY

Chapter 3 describes the major methodology used to collect the data which will be used to answer the hypotheses. In some theses, *several* methods may be used because 'increasingly authors and researchers who work in organisations and with managers argue that one should attempt to mix methods to some extent, because it provides more perspectives on the phenomena being studied' (Easterby-Smith 1991, p. 31). But within the time and other resource constraints of most theses, I suggest that there will usually be only one *major* methodology which suits the research problem and associated research gaps uncovered in Chapter 2. Other methodologies would be used in a *secondary* role to help formulate research issues (for example, some interviews used to help design a survey's questionnaire could be described in Chapter 2 if they helped to formulate propositions/hypotheses, or in Chapter 3 if they helped in developing the operational definitions of constructs) or to slightly extend or generalise the findings of the main method (for example, some interviews could be used to confirm an unexpected result and could be described in Chapter 4 or 5). So, Chapter 3 usually centres on the major methodology of the research.

Level of detail in Chapter 3. Chapter 3 about data collection and analysis must be written so another trained researcher could replicate the research. That is, there must be enough detail for 'a reasonably knowledgeable colleague' to repeat the data collection and analysis (Lindsay 1995, p. 14). But there is a second consideration involved in deciding how much detail to put in the chapter—the candidate must also show the examiner that the candidate understands the methodology. The candidate can assume that the examiner has a good undergraduate training in the methodology and two to three years research experience (Brown 1996), but the examiner cannot assume the candidate has the same training. Thus candidates will have to provide enough detail to show the examiner that the candidate also knows the body of knowledge about the methodology and its procedures, even if it is in only a couple of sentences with references. If the technique is an advanced one, like structural equation modelling that is only covered in postgraduate courses, one or two of the examiners may have to be 'brought up to speed' on the technique, and so more material will be necessary in the thesis about the technique and why it was used, than when a basic technique is being used.

That is, examiners need to be assured that *all* critical procedures and processes have been followed. For example, a thesis using regression as the prime methodology should include details of the pilot study, handling of response bias and tests for assumptions of regression. A thesis using factor analysis would cover preliminary tests such as Bartlett's and scree tests and discuss core issues such as the sample size and method of rotation. A thesis using a survey would discuss the usual core steps of population, sampling frame, sample design, sample size and so on in order.

In addition to critical procedures and processes, candidates must show familiarity with controversies and positions taken by authorities. That is, candidates must show familiarity with the body of knowledge about the methodology, just as they did with the bodies of knowledge in Chapter 2 (Phillips & Pugh 2000). An example of this familiarity for candidates using a qualitative methodology would be an awareness of how validity and reliability are viewed in qualitative research, for example, in a discussion of how the ideas about them in Easterby-Smith et al. (2008) and Healy and Perry (2000) were used in the research. For another example, merely providing details of the telephone survey used for the research is inadequate, because the advantages and disadvantages of *other* types of surveys must also be discussed and the choice of a telephone survey justified. Another example would be to show awareness of the controversy about whether a Likert scale is interval or merely ordinal and justify adoption of interval scales by reference to authorities like a candidate who said:

> A number of reasons account for this use of Likert scales. First, these scales have been found to communicate interval properties to the respondent, and therefore produce data that can be assumed to be intervally scaled (Madsen 1989; Schertzer & Kernan 1985). Second,

in the marketing literature Likert scales are almost always treated as interval scales (for example, Kohli 1989).

Yet another example would be to show awareness of the controversy about the number of points in a Likert scale by referring to authorities' discussions of the issue, like Armstrong (1985) and Neuman (2007).

This issue of how much detail and what detail to put into the methodology chapter is not a clear cut one. The candidate has to steer a fine line between giving the examiners a 'tutorial' about the methodology (which the examiners definitely do not need for the reasons noted above), and merely telling the story of what was done to collect the data and analyse it. That is, the thesis writer has to demonstrate research training and justify the steps undertaken but without boring the examiner. Three ways of demonstrating this knowledge and training without 'loading an undergraduate's tutorial' on to the examiners are: using the past tense as much as possible, frequently referencing literature about the methodology, and describing what was done in the jargon of that literature. The following example shows how this demonstration of knowledge and training could be done. The example's sentences about what was done are written in the past tense, but clearly demonstrate that the writer is familiar with the methodology literature that is lavishly referenced, including its jargon:

> The fourth issue about this research design concerned sample design. Sample design involved the selection of a technique to choose elements from the population of interest and involved the choice of either probability or non-probability design (Emory & Cooper 1991; Frazer & Lawley 2000). Determination of sample design followed five steps synthesised from the literature that are discussed next (Malhotra et al. 1996; Smith 2000; Rubin 1996).

The candidate must not only show that they know the appropriate body of knowledge about procedures as noted above, but must also provide *some evidence* that the correct procedures have been followed. For example, dates of interviews or survey mailings should be provided. Appendices to the thesis should contain copies of instruments used and instruments referred to, and some examples of computer printouts; however, well-constructed tables of results in Chapter 4 should be adequate for the reader to determine correctness of analysis, and so *all* computer printouts do not need to be in the appendices (although they should be kept by the candidate just in case the examiner asks for them). Note that appendices should contain all information to which an intensely interested reader needs to refer; a careful examiner should not be expected to go to a library or write to the candidate's university to check some points.

All these details of the methodology are required whether a qualitative or quantitative research methodology is used (Yin 2009), and Table 5 shows the position of each of these within the pathway of a unified qualitative or quantitative thesis. A qualitative thesis may contain even *more* details than a quantitative one, for a qualitative researcher may influence subjects more—for example, how subjects were chosen, how they answered, and how notes and/or recordings were used. Moreover, the candidate should occasionally use 'I' in the methodology chapter when a qualitative methodology is used in the thesis, to describe what they actually did in the field, so as to reflect an awareness that the researcher cannot be independent of the field data. Indeed, perhaps a qualitative researcher could briefly describe themselves in the validity and reliability section of this chapter, as a way of trying to make themselves and the reader aware of values that may bias their findings. For example, one researcher wrote (Pettigrew 1999, p. 151):

> At the time of the data collection, the researcher was self-described as a white, Australian, late-twenties, middle class, non-beer drinking, non-smoking, tertiary-qualified, married female. Numerous preconceptions came along with these characteristics.

Table 5 — Aspects of a unified thesis

QUALITATIVE RESEARCH	QUANTITATIVE RESEARCH
Research problem: how? why?	Research problem: who (how many)? what (how much)?
Literature review: exploratory—what are the variables involved? constructs are messy research issues are developed	Literature review: explanatory—what are the relationships between the variables which have been previously identified and measured? hypotheses are developed
Paradigm: critical realism/interpretive	Paradigm: positivist
Methodology: for example, case study research or action research	Methodology: for example, survey or experiment

Incidentally, I think that as rough rules of thumb, PhD research could require at least 350 respondents in a quantitative survey or at least 15 to 35 interviews in four to twelve qualitative case studies. In contrast, honours research could require about 50 to 100 respondents in a survey, or at least four to five interviews, in four to five case studies. Master's research could lie between these two limits.

A rigorous methodology. In brief, Chapter 3 describes the methodology adopted (for example, a mail survey and a particular need for achievement instrument), in a far more detailed way than in the introductory description of Section 1.5. For a start, the operational definitions of constructs used in questionnaires or interviews to measure an hypothesised relationship will be described and justified, for example, how an interval scale was devised for the questionnaire. Note that some authorities consider that PhD research should rarely use a previously developed instrument in a new application without extensive justification—they would argue that an old instrument in a new application is merely Master's level work and is not appropriate for PhD work. However, often *parts* of the PhD instrument could have been developed by authorities (for example, a need for achievement instrument), but those parts must still be justified through previous studies of reliability and validity and/or be piloted to the PhD candidate's requirements in order to assess their reliability and validity, and alternatives must be carefully considered and rejected. Any revisions to the authority's instrument must be identified and justified. Alternatively, multi-item measures could be developed for constructs that have been previously measured with a single item, to increase reliability and validity. It can be argued that an old instrument in a new application will be an original investigation, and so a new or partly-new instrument is not an absolute necessity for PhD research (Phillips, E. 1992, pers. comm.). Nevertheless, others recommend some qualitative pilot studies before an old instrument is used—they will confirm its appropriateness and may suggest additional questions that help develop new ideas for the thesis, thus reducing the risk that an examiner will disapprove of the thesis.

Let us turn to more precise details of Chapter 3. The chapter should have separate sections to cover, for both qualitative and quantitative research:

- *justification for the methodology* in terms of the research problem and the literature review, for example, a qualitative methodology often requires a research problem involving people's constructions of meanings which have not previously been explored (Hassard 1990)—Yin (2009, p. 8) has a table which might help in writing about this justification;

incidentally, recent theses are showing an awareness of the strengths and weaknesses of the positivist and interpretive paradigms as a basis for discussing choice of methodology (Easterby-Smith et al. 2008)
- the *unit of analysis* and subjects or sources of data, for example, explicit reference to steps such as deciding the population, the sampling frame and the sample, and the sample size; for case study research, these are discussed in Perry (1998b)
- *instruments* or procedures used to collect data, including how the dependent variable was measured, details of pilot studies and explicit concern about specific procedures used to handle internal and external validity (as in Yin 2009, p. 41; Parkhe 1993, pp. 260-261; Lincoln & Guba 1985, pp. 290-294); note that the boundaries of external validity were *implicitly* addressed in Sections 1.2, 1.6 and 1.7
- *administration* of instruments or procedures (for example, when, where and who, non-response bias (which is a very important issue and is discussed in Armstrong & Overton (1977)), response rates, dates and protocols of interviews (Yin 2009), so that the research is reliable, that is, it could be repeated
- *limitations* of the methodology, for example, practical limitations on the sampling frame or size of questionnaire in survey research might be clarified and justified (for example, some types of respondents might have been missed because of their religious beliefs), and Parkhe (1993, p. 255) discusses some possible limitations of the case study methodology which should have been addressed in a thesis.
- any special or unusual treatments of data before it was analysed (for example, special scoring of answers to a survey question)
- evidence that the *assumptions* of analytical techniques were met, for example, that the sample sizes were large enough and assumptions of normality were tested for (Hair at al. (1995) discusses these assumptions for each multivariate technique)
- *validity and reliability* issues and how they were addressed; in qualitative research, these issues could be discussed in the way formulated in Healy and Perry (2000)
- computer programs used to *analyse the data*, with justifications for their use (for example, why chi-square was used instead of a Wilcoxon test)—this may require a brief description of the type of data and some appropriate references where similar procedures had been used in similar circumstances
- *ethical* issues based around the concept of informed consent.

In addition to the above items, Chapter 3 should show that other variables that might influence results were controlled in the research design (and so held at one or two set levels) or properly measured for later inclusion in statistical analyses (for example, as a variable in regression analysis). This point is an important consideration for examiners.

To fully demonstrate competence in research procedures, the statistical forms of hypotheses could be explicitly developed and justified in a thesis, even though such precision is often not required in far shorter journal articles describing similar research. Some candidates are confused between the more abstract *propositions* sometimes developed towards the end of a literature review and statistical *hypotheses*. The propositions in Chapter 2 are framed in the form *with which most experts would agree*, for example, that smoking causes cancer. In contrast, the statistical hypotheses developed in Chapters 3 or 4 are in a form that is directly ready for statistical testing and have a format of a formal null hypothesis of zero difference, for example, that there is no association between smoking and cancer, and an alternative hypothesis of some difference. The null and the alternative hypotheses could be either directional or not. A directional hypothesis will require different forms of statistical tests of significance than a non-directional hypothesis; for example, the use of a directional hypothesis allows a one-tailed test of significance.

The list of Chapter 3's details above noted some ethical procedures and the penultimate section of Chapter 3 should cover them. The ultimate section is the conclusion. By the way, it is an ethical position of theses that the writer has verified that a reference does actually say what the thesis says it does. For example, if a thesis says Smith (1995) referred to the sample size for a multivariate technique, the candidate must have read Smith's article, or at the very least read an abstract which clearly confirms that Smith did discuss sample sizes in the way the candidate says Smith did.

In summary, writing Chapter 3 is analogous to an accountant laying an 'audit trail'—the candidate should treat the examiner as an accountant treats an auditor, showing they know and can justify the correct procedures and providing evidence that they have been followed.

3.4 CHAPTER 4 ANALYSIS OF DATA

Chapter 4 presents patterns of results and analyses them for their relevance to the research issues or propositions/hypotheses. Frequent summary tables and figures of results are essential, so that readers can easily see patterns in the mass of data presented in the chapter. Tables of statistical data are presented in quantitative research and matrices are used in qualitative research (Miles & Huberman 1985). But note that an examiner should not *have* to look at tables and figures to be able follow your arguments. If there is an important point in a table or figure, you have to incorporate it into your text—the examiner should not have to do your work by ferreting for points in tables and figures. That is, an examiner should be able to pass a thesis without having to look at any of its tables or figures, if they happen to be in a hurry. Similarly, tables and figures should be able to be read somewhat independently of the text, so ensure the titles of tables and figures are rather long and self-explanatory, and any symbols in a table are explained in a note to the table. That is, a table should be understood by someone who has not read the text. By the way, a table has rows and columns and a figure does not.

Consider tables and figures in a bit more detail. A table or figure should go immediately after a paragraph that first refers to it, if possible. But a table or figure that is less than one page in length should not be broken up onto separate pages, so the table or figure may sometimes have to go after the paragraph that follows the paragraph where it is first referred to. Occasionally, a table or figure may be too big to fit on one page; when this space problem occurs, start the following page(s) with an *abbreviated* title like 'Table 2.9 (continued)'. Titles at the top of *all* tables or figures in a document like a thesis should be in the same font and be smaller than 12 point—I suggest you use an 11 point font for all these titles; use bold for the name but not for the number, and do not have a full stop at the end of the title. In turn, the words and numbers within a table or figure should be in a smaller font than that of the title of the table or figure—I suggest you use 10 point font. Notes and sources at the bottom of a table or figure (with a full stop at their end) should be the same as all the other words within the table or figure, that is, 10 point font if you follow my suggestions above.

Let us now return to the structure of Chapter 4. Chapter 4 should be clearly organised. The introduction has the normal link to the previous chapter, chapter objective and outline, but also often has basic, *justified* assumptions like significance levels and whether one- or two-tailed tests were used. The introduction of Chapter 4 may be different from introductions of other chapters because it refers to the following chapter as well as to the preceding chapter, for Chapter 5 will discuss the findings of Chapter 4 within the context of the literature. Without this warning, an examiner may wonder why some of the implications of the results are not drawn out in Chapter 4. Chapter 4 should be restricted to presentation and analysis of the collected data, without drawing general conclusions or comparing results to those of other researchers who were discussed in Chapter 2. That is, although Chapter 4 may contain references to the literature about methodologies, it should not contain references to any other literature. If the chapter does include references to other literature, then later, the more complete discussion of Chapter 5 will be undesirably repetitive and confused. In any case, it is traditional in science to separate discussion of the results from the discussion of their significance, to preserve objectivity: 'To qualify each result, or group of results, with comments and comparisons gives the strong impression that you are trying to influence the objective judgment of the reader' (Lindsay 1995, p. 17).

After the introduction, descriptive data about the subjects is usually provided, for example, their gender or industry in survey research, or a brief description of case study organisations in case study research. This description helps to assure the examiner that the candidate has a 'good feel' for the data, that is, they know good researchers have to 'handle their own rats' (Frost & Stablein 1992, p. 271).

Then the data for each research issue or proposition is usually presented, in the same order as they were presented in Chapters 2 and 3 (and will be later in Sections 5.2 and 5.3). Structuring the data analysis around the research issues or propositions/hypotheses will ensure the candidate does not make the mistake of falling in love with the data (Brown 1996) and telling the reader how beautiful all of the data is—the data analysis must focus *only* on solving the research problem by looking at each research issue or hypothesis in turn. Sensitivity analyses of findings to possible errors in data (for example, ordinal rather than assumed interval scales) should be included. If qualitative research is being done, an additional section could possibly be provided for data that was collected that does not fit into the research issue categories developed in the literature review of Chapter 2.

The general rule in reporting your findings is to give the *forest first and then the trees*. Go through each hypothesis/research issue in these six steps of Bem (2002) (all the quantitative examples below are extracted directly from Bem, with only the one qualitative example added):

1. Remind the reader of the conceptual hypothesis or issue you are considering. Note that this is a *conceptual statement* of the hypothesis or question. After that, look at the precise aspects or measurement that is going to be discussed next—this is an *operational statement* of the hypothesis or question.
2. Next, tell the reader what the answer is, in English without

numbers. You do this *before* going into the details—remember: a thesis is not a whodunit. For example, 'Men do, in fact, cry more profusely than the women'.
3. Then, and only then, speak about the *actual results* in numbers for quantitative research, or general terms with numbers inside brackets for qualitative research. One example is: 'Thus the men in all four conditions produced an average of 1.4 cc more tears than the women ($F(1,112) = 5.79$, $p < .025$.).' A qualitative example elaborated on in the third paragraph below is: Most respondents thought shipping was not important because schedules were reliable (row 2 of Table 4.3). 'Thank goodness the unions are tame' (A2). 'No worries—we have good port agents and shipping lines' (B1).
4. Now you may *elaborate or qualify* the overall conclusion if necessary, for example: 'Only in the father-watching condition did the men fail to produce more tears than the women, but a specific test of this effect failed to reach significance ($t = 1.58$, $p < 0.12$.).'
5. End each section of the results with a *summary* of where things stand: 'Thus, except for the father-watching condition, which will be discussed below, the hypothesis that men cry more than women in response to visually-depicted grief appears to receive strong support.'
6. Lead into the next section of the results with a smooth transition sentence if there is a clear linkage between this and the next section (do not do this lead-in here if there is no clear linkage): 'Men may thus be more expressive than women in the domain of negative emotion, but are they more expressive in the domain of positive emotion? Table 2 shows they are not...'

In all of Chapter 4, the data should not be merely presented without analysis, with the examiner being expected to analyse it. One way of ensuring adequate analysis is done by the candidate in a **quantitative** thesis is to have interpretive words describing the data followed by numbers placed in brackets, for example, 'most survey respondents (69 percent)...' For the same reason, test statistics, degrees of freedom, sample size and p values should be explained in words that show the candidate knows what they mean, followed by their values placed in brackets (to allow the examiner to check test statistics details in tables, if they wish). Note that some statisticians prefer not to accept the null hypothesis just because it is *not rejected* (because the Type II error involved in acceptance is not known, although the Type I error involved in rejection is), hence the practical implications of a statistical test involving no significant difference between test statistics must be made explicit from the statistically expressed result, that is, it should not be not confused with the statistical result. An example of all this appropriate analysis is:

> Question 9 explored attitudes to product quality and respondent's answers are summarised in Table 4.6. Most respondents (59.2 percent) agreed that the product quality was important, but a sizeable minority (27.8 percent) had no view about product quality—a somewhat surprising finding which will also be discussed within the context of the literature in Section 5.4.3... A t-test was used to discern the relationship between attitudes to product quality and price (Section 4.9), because both were measured with an interval scale. No significant difference between the means of attitudes to the two variables was found ($t = 1.56$, dof = 23, 25; $p = 0.35$). A practical implication of this finding is that the shoppers considered product quality and price separately.

Some researchers in reputable journals do not provide precise p values when reporting the analysis of their data and merely say whether the test statistic is significant at a certain level, for example, '$p<0.05$'. However, other researchers consider that this procedure does not provide all the information offered by modern computer programs and so prefer to report the precise p value, as was done in the example above. One compromise between these two positions would be to use a particular level in the text, for example, '$p<0.01$', and have the precise p levels listed in a table.

The discussion of results above was based on quantitative analysis. Reporting the analysis of **qualitative** data is slightly different. Firstly, the overall patterns in the data are presented, with *reasons* for those patterns occurring included. There is no reference to numbers of respondents or cases here, in the discussion of a finding, because the sample will have been chosen in a purposive way and so there can be no claim for statistical representativeness (Patton 2002). Then the reader could be referred to a matrix of the findings (Miles & Huberman 1994) where more details can be found to support the claim that the pattern in the data does indeed exist. Finally, specific examples and quotations to further corroborate the existence of the pattern in the data are presented. A brief example of this presentation of qualitative findings is:

> Most respondents thought shipping was not important because schedules were reliable (row 2 of Table 4.3). 'Thank goodness the

unions are tame' (A2). 'No worries—we have good port agents and shipping lines' (B1).

Presenting analyses of qualitative data can be difficult because *patterns* in the wordy data must be made clear without overlooking the *particulars* in the data that provide the in-depth strength of qualitative data. These paragraphs from the introduction to a thesis' data analysis chapter outline these two considerations and how they were addressed in the chapter:

> Two considerations made it difficult to blend qualitative details and synthesised patterns in the data within this chapter; that is, blend the 'wood' and the 'trees'. The patterns in the data that explained why and how the world operates is the 'wood' and was the primary concern of this chapter. However, details of the 'trees' also had to be presented in this chapter to confirm the trustworthiness of the patterns described. First, because this research was an in-depth investigation of a complex and under-researched area, this chapter had to be quite detailed in some parts of its analysis, for example, there are matrices for each type of finding (Miles and Huberman 1994) that show the results for each case. Secondly, the requirement for trustworthiness in qualitative research made it necessary to provide detailed quotations and other evidence for the patterns found in the data, together with the sources of the quotations. In brief, patterns had to be synthesised from the data without losing sight of the rich, qualitative sources on which they were based.
>
> To draw these considerations together, this chapter is clearly structured around the three research issues and there are frequent summaries of the patterns of data being uncovered, with supporting quotations. In particular, the tables and figures are critical to following the patterns being uncovered in the data, for readers can gain an overall picture of the findings from them. In particular, Figure 4.9 summarises the findings examined throughout the whole chapter and so provides an overview of the whole chapter.

Whether the data is qualitative or quantitative, all patterns of results in Chapter 4 must be supported by the evidence unearthed through the procedures described in Chapter 3. That is, a reader should be able to check findings by looking at tables or figures. So each and every table or figure should be referred to in the text in the body of the chapter, with the reason for its presence. As the example in the previous paragraph showed, a topic should be introduced in words and the main findings presented; *then* the table or figure referred to and evidence from it should be introduced in one or two sentences; and then the highlights of the table or figure should be discussed more fully, together with a brief description of what the reader will look for in the table or figure when they turn to it. In other words, a reader should not be expected to develop the links between the words in Chapter 4 and a table or figure by themselves. Indeed, the reader should be able to grasp the meaning by reading *either* the words in the text or the tables and figures without reference to the other.

All tables and figures should have a number and title at the top and their source at the bottom, for example, 'Source: analysis of survey data'. The title of a table or graph should contain enough information that its findings can be discerned without referring to the text, but be limited to one line; for example, 'Relationship marketing propensity among respondents is similar despite cultural differences'. If no source is listed, the examiner will assume the researcher's mind is the source, but a listing such as 'Source: developed for this research from Chapter 2' might reinforce the originality of the candidate's work.

3.5 CHAPTER 5 CONCLUSIONS AND IMPLICATIONS

The research data has been analysed in Chapter 4 but what does it all mean? The sections in Chapter 5 answer that question. Chapter 5 uncovers all the contributions of the research project and so is the most important chapter of the thesis; after ensuring the methodology and research processes are sound, the examiners will spend much time studying Chapter 5. But the chapter is often marked by fatigue, and so Phillips and Pugh (2000, p. 56) note that the chapter's 'inadequacy is the single most common reason for requiring candidates to resubmit their theses after first presentation'. Thus the candidate must discover springs of interest and creativity to make their Chapter 5 worthy of the rest of the thesis, and make it clearly show that the research does make a distinct contribution to the body of knowledge.

Section 5.1 Introduction

Do remember that the introduction to Section 5.1 is longer than the introduction of other chapters because it refers to all the other chapters and not just the previous one, as noted in the part of Section 2.1 of this book chapter above titled 'Links between chapters'. A jigsaw puzzle analogy is useful for understanding what the start of Chapter 5 is about. Research begins like a jumbled jigsaw puzzle about the research problem. Chapter 2's literature review starts putting the pieces together to try to uncover a picture, but shows that some pieces are missing and so the complete picture cannot be known. Then Chapters 3 and 4 describe the hunt for the missing pieces and the matching together of a few, newly found pieces.

Finally, Chapter 5 returns to the puzzle, briefly summarising what the early picture looked like at the end of Chapter 2 and then explaining how the new and the old pieces fit to make the *whole* picture clear. By the way, we have found that Chapter 5 should note the date when the literature review closed and explicitly noting that *more recent* literature is included in this chapter, along these lines:

> This section presents the conclusions of this research—the findings in Chapter 4 will be fitted into the literature reviewed in Chapter 2 to identify the contributions. However, the literature review was completed in June 2008, because data began to be gathered at that time to investigate the research issues raised by the literature. Therefore, more recent literature will be incorporated into this chapter to assist in the discussion of the findings. (This procedure of incorporating recent literature into the final chapter and not in Chapter 2 is supported by Murray (2006, p. 238)—'you can be justifiably explicit with your readers about where you can draw the line on new research').

By the way, there should be about four or five top journals that could conceivably publish articles about your PhD research. You should check issues of those journals *in the year in which you will submit the PhD*, for articles that have even distant links to your thesis, and cite and reference them. Doing this is useful training for your later academic writing career, as you will go through this process when you submit an article to any journal.

After setting up Chapter 5 in this way, we immediately address the issue of the research's contributions. Identifying what is a distinct contribution to knowledge can bewilder some candidates, as Phillips (1992, p. 128) found in a survey of Australian academics and candidates, and as we noted in the paragraphs dealing with Section 1.2 above. Consequently, we make it clear to the examiner what we mean by a 'contribution' by having a table at the start of the final chapter which lists the seven or so 'new' themes of the thesis for each research issue/proposition and notes the degree that the extant literature had explicitly addressed them, with words like 'to some extent', 'to a very small extent', and 'none'. Then we introduce the terms we will use in the final chapter to describe contributions along these lines:

> Some of this research's findings do confirm expectations from the extant literature but it is the first time that this has been done for Australian situations. These will be called advances on that

previous research in this chapter—they are of interest because they add a new depth to our understanding of the phenomenon. However, these advances will not be called contributions in this chapter because our focus will be on more important contributions or additions to knowledge arising from findings about:

- disconfirmations of expectations derived in Chapter 2 from the literature, indicated by the themes with a 'to some extent' entry in the table;
- areas about which there were some speculations in the literature but no empirical testing, indicated by the themes with a 'to a very small extent' entry in the table; and
- new areas which had not been raised in the previous literature, indicated by themes with a 'none' entry in the table.

Section 5.2 Conclusions about research issues or propositions/hypotheses
After the introduction to Chapter 5, findings for each research issue or proposition are summarised from Chapter 4 and explained within the context of this and prior research examined in Chapter 2; for example, with which of the researchers discussed in Chapter 2 does this research agree or disagree, how and why? For example, the disagreement might be because some previous research was done in Asia and this research was done in Australia.

This disagreement suggests the PhD research is making a contribution to knowledge and this *contribution of the research* should be clearly developed. Each research issue or proposition would have its own subsection, that is, Section 5.2.1, 5.2.2 and so on, and each of these sections will have a reference to the appropriate section of Chapter 4 so that the examiner can clearly see that the conclusions come from the findings in Chapter 4. Note that the verb 'confirms' is rarely used to show the relationship between the data and the literature ; the verb confirms is too lame—other, better verbs are 'add', 'complement', 'extend', 'expand', 'enrich', 'build on' and 'explain' (and 'contribute', too, of course).

For each research issue/proposition, the agreement or disagreement of the results of a numbered section in Chapter 4 with the literature should be made clear and the reason for disagreement thought through. Of course, each section will also have many references to the writers discussed in Chapter 2 because this chapter's primary aim is to show how the findings in the previous chapter fit into the body of knowledge. A brief example of one of these discussions is:

The final set of factors in the initial conceptual framework of this research illustrated in Figure 2.10 was the strategic objectives of the firm. The interaction between entry mode choice and strategic objectives has attracted considerable attention in the literature (Jones 1991; Anderson & Gatignon 1986; Hwang 1988; Hill et al, 1990). For example, Minor, Wu and Choi (1991) argue that entry mode choice is based on strategic objectives when considered in tandem with...

This research had varied findings about these factors. Section 4.3.5's findings were that innovation learning and whether firms consider a global strategy are unimportant. These findings are inconsistent with the literature. The reasons for this inconsistency appear to be the small size of the firms in this survey and their industry. Jones (1991) surveyed firms with turnovers above $1 million in the pharmaceutical industry, and Hwang (1988) surveyed... In contrast, Australian small jewelers are... Presumably, they are more entrepreneurial and have less at stake than larger firms and...

Here is a longer example of a discussion of how the findings fit into the literature, from the Discussion section of an article (Ozcan & Eisenhradt 2009, p. 270; bold and Comments added). Note in particular that the example shows:

- How very closely linked are the particulars of the findings to details of the ideas in the literature and how those findings make contributions to the literature.
- There are lots of citations.
- How very well structured the discussion is, with lots of signposts. For example, the contributions are mentioned up front at the beginning of the section. Then the first contribution is discussed, and this discussion goes through point after point; you could perhaps say 'Firstly,.. On the one hand,.. On the other hand,... Finally, ...'
- How previous literature is not denigrated in any way—this research fits around previous researchers and extends them, it does not contradict them. Essentially, the purpose of the Discussion section is to show how the findings are new and how they fit into existing literature.

The example is:

EXCERPT FROM OZCAN & EISENHRADT (2009, P. 270; WITH EMPHASES IN ADDED ITALICS)	COMMENT
We add to *inter-organizational network theory and the study of strategy within entrepreneurial firms* by specifying a theoretical framework for *how* firms create high-performing portfolios.	The research problem theory (in italics) where a contribution is made, is clearly stated. This is the finding that was established in the previous Data analysis/Results/Findings section – those findings built a framework for how firms create high-performing portfolio.
[Previous] research has identified the attributes of high-performing portfolios (Baum et al., 2000; Uzzi, 1997) and given a deterministic account of how networks and portfolios evolve (Gulati & Gargiulo, 1999; Powell et al.,1996). But this work leaves open the question of how firms actually originate high-performing portfolios.	Previous research is briefly noted and the GAP stated.
Addressing this gap, we explored how closely comparable rivals began their portfolios. The emergent theoretical framework explains the strategic actions by which firms originate high-performing portfolios. It makes **fundamental contributions** in the areas of network agency and strategy.	This whole Discussion section is going to be about CONTRIBUTIONS—that is what a Discussion should focus on.

The example (contd.)

EXCERPT FROM OZCAN & EISENHRADT (2009, P. 270; WITH EMPHASES IN ADDED ITALICS)	COMMENT
Our study offers *several insights* for inter-organizational network theory regarding the origins of high-performing portfolios. *A key insight* is that executives in firms with high-performing portfolios visualize their portfolios in the context of an entire network, not as a series of single ties… A *second insight regarding high-performing portfolios* is the crucial logic of simultaneous multiple ties. … Firms can, thus, synchronize and reinforce their tie execution by cocreating well-integrated industry architectures (Proposition 1), intricately synchronizing joint activities such as new products (Proposition 2), and combining information sources to better understand industry uncertainties (Proposition 3)…	Details of the contributions are made explicit in easily-followed writing, and are related to the propositions/research issues that guided data collection and analysis, and provided a structure to the presentation of the findings in the previous Data analysis/Results/Findings section. Note that the contributions are to the research problem of *interorganizational network theory and the study of strategy within entrepreneurial firms*, and not to parent theories—the parent theories are covered in the later implications section.

Section 5.3 Conclusions about the research problem

Based on Section 5.2, implications of the research for furthering understanding of the research problem are explored in Section 5.3. That is, the section goes beyond the mere number-crunching of Chapter 4 and incorporates qualitative findings about the research problem developed during the research, including those insights discovered during interviews in qualitative research which had never even been considered in the literature reviewed in Chapter 2. Again the contribution of the research to the body of knowledge should be clearly developed.

You are warned that examiners are careful that conclusions in Section 5.2 and 5.3 are based on *findings* alone, and so will dispute conclusions not clearly based on the research results. That is, there is a difference between the *conclusions* of the research findings in Sections 5.2 and 5.3 and *implications* drawn from them later in Sections 5.4 and 5.5. For example, if a qualitative methodology is used with its limited claims for statistical generalisability, the conclusions must refer specifically to the people or enterprises interviewed in the past or to the context of the research setting, for example, 'the Hong Kong managers placed small value on advertising' is appropriate but 'Chinese managers place small value on price' is not.

This Section 5.3 on conclusions about the research problem section may sometimes be quite small if the propositions/hypotheses or research issues dealt with in the previous sections cover the area of the research problem in a comprehensive way. Nevertheless, the section is usually worth including for it provides a conclusion to the *whole* research effort. Thus it is advisable to try to put together a final *conceptual* framework that encapsulates the achievements of the thesis. For example, a thesis that used structural equation modelling could present the final model chosen from the rival models in Chapter 4, without the coefficients that cluttered up the many figures of the several models in Chapter 4.

Moreover, I suggest that this section conclude with a summary listing of the contributions of the research, if that is not clear from the discussion in the previous sections of this chapter. As noted earlier, the examiner is looking for these contributions and it may make his or her task easier if the candidate explicitly lists them after introducing them in earlier parts of this chapter. This section should be especially important for qualitative, theory-building research for it will show the final theory that is developed and have a model of its conceptual framework in a figure, and also possibly develop some propositions/hypotheses which later researchers can use to test the theory.

If one or more of the models developed in Chapter 2 have to be modified because of the research findings, then the modified model should be developed in Section 5.3, with the modifications clearly marked in bold on the figure. Indeed, development of a modified model of the classification or analytical models developed in Chapter 2 is an excellent summary of how the research has added to the body of knowledge, and is strongly recommended.

Section 5.4 Implications for theory
Based on the sections above, implications of the research for furthering understanding of the research problem are explored next. This section often focusses on the possible effects of the findings on the *parent* theories. In effect, the *full* picture of the research's findings within the body of knowledge is provided in Section 5.4, that is, it provides the theoretical implications of the research.

This section aims to convince examiners that the findings of PhD research have not only made a significant contribution to knowledge in its research problem theory as outlined in Sections 5.2 and 5.3, but also has implications (that is, speculations) for the wider body of knowledge, including the parent theories of Chapter 2 and even to other related theories or discipline that were not even mentioned among the few parent theories of Chapter 2. The parent theories are those that are the *direct* background to the conceptual framework developed at the end of Chapter 2, but there may be other theories that could benefit from the findings of this research; the broad range of disciplines mentioned in Section 1.1 might suggest some of these related theories.

For example, in a PhD thesis with a research problem involving customer service, Section 5.4 might refer not only to the parent theories of services marketing but also to consumer behavior, personality characteristics and psychological motivations. And in a PhD thesis about international education, Section 5.4 might refer to international marketing and services marketing.

Here is an example of the implications for theory section of an article (Ozcan & Eisenhardt 2009, p. 270); it followed the contributions to the research problem theory section of the previous example above with insights for the parent theories:

EXCERPT FROM OZCAN & EISENHRADT (2009, P. 270; WITH EMPHASES IN ADDED ITALICS)	COMMENT
Resource dependence and *social embeddedness* are the two primary theoretical explanations of tie formation and network evolution. Our granular view of portfolios offers insights for both theories.	The two theories in italics are the two parent theories. The research adds insights to them, in addition to the contributions to the research problem theory noted above. The 'granular' view refers to the findings and their contributions to the research problem theory described above.
First, this article contributes to **resource dependence theory** by enriching its core construct, interdependence. On the one hand, we *affirm* the central role of interdependence in tie formation [in previous research]. On the other hand, we *offer a richer conception* of interdependence. In prior research, interdependence is often assumed to be an exogenous and stable property of dyadic relationships (Casciaro & Piskorski, 2005 …). *In contrast*, we argue that executives can proactively create a vision of interdependence (i.e., industry architecture) that is unique and advantageous to multiple types of firms. Thus, interdependence can be multilateral and socially constructed, not just fixed and dyadic (Casciaro & Piskorski, 2005).	These insights are implications for the parent theory of resource dependence. Note how the previous literature is acknowledged and how this research has politely extended those previous understandings. For example, it begins by *affirming* previous research about central role of interdependence in tie formation, but then *offers* a richer conception of interdependence. The aim is to acknowledge and build on the foundations of previous research, not to demolish those foundations.

(contd)

EXCERPT FROM OZCAN & EISENHRADT (2009, P. 270; WITH EMPHASES IN ADDED ITALICS)	COMMENT
We contribute to **social network theory** by sharpening its focal concept of embeddedness. On the one hand, we *expand the concept* of embeddedness to include the possibility that the prospect of ties can be used to form ties. Prior research has emphasized the importance of existing direct and indirect ties for verifying the quality of partners (Gulati, 1995; Hallen, 2008). *We complement this understanding* by arguing that firms are sometimes interested enough in each other to require only limited verification of quality in the form of simply having another interested potential partner (i.e., the prospect of a tie).	These insights are implications for the second **parent theory** of social embeddedness. Note, again, how the previous literature is acknowledged and how this research has politely extended those previous understandings.

Section 5.5 Implications for policy and practice

After all the literature above is dealt with, practical implications for private sector managers are covered in Section 5.5.1 and implications for public sector analysts and managers are covered in Section 5.5.2. Needs for training or new government policies are often raised here. Examiners may be impressed if this section develops a checklist of procedures for managers which incorporates the research findings, and this checklist may help to fulfill justification iv of Section 1.3.

Section 5.6 Implications for methodology

This section is optional and has the writer's reflections on the methodology used. For example, it could discuss what parts were especially successful and what parts were especially difficult, what procedures had to be developed that were not previously described in the literature about the methodology, and if any of that literature was especially useful or misleading. The section normally takes up only about half a page or so.

Section 5.7 Limitations and implications for further research
Section 1.7 has previously outlined major delimitations of the research that were a deliberate part of the research (for example, industry boundaries to the research problem). This section discusses other limitations that became apparent during the progress of the research, for example, questionnaire results may indicate that age of respondents is a limitation. Sometimes this section can be quite short, after all, most of these limitations were dealt with in Chapter 3. Indeed, do not make too much of any limitations, for too much discussion here will make the examiner think the research was poorly designed and any conclusions are not worth awarding a degree for—it has been a poorly designed 'house of cards'. Nevertheless, you do have to be honest and admit any limitations that were uncovered along the way.

So this section should show that the limitations are acknowledged, but that they do not detract from the significance of the findings. Indeed, the section could begin with a brief statement about the strengths of the research, for example, the size of the sample and the unusual methodology. Then the section could discuss some limitations like the use of perceptions in data collection rather than figures, the use of a convenience sample and the use of cross-sectional rather than longitudinal data. Finally, the section could end with a paragraph that the strengths of the study remain for the limitations do not detract from them but merely provide platforms for future research (which are addressed in the next section). Then the section adds some paragraphs to help candidates and other researchers in selecting and designing future research (some of the suggestions would flow from the limitations above, that is, suggest how the limitations could be addressed in future). Further research could refer to both topics and to methodologies or to both. A case research methodology thesis could mention the need for positivism survey research to generalise the findings. Removing some delimitations mentioned and justified in Section 1.7 usually provides opportunities for further research, for example, similar research could be done in different regions or countries, in different industries and with different levels of management. This section might be enhanced by the development of the actual propositions/hypotheses or research issues that a follow up researcher could use to start their research design stage.

Section 5.8 Conclusion
A final paragraph or two could summarise and tie the whole thesis together. Writers usually look back at the research problem of the thesis and try to show that the problem has been answered. For example, a thesis might end with 'The literature suggests that the marketing/entrepreneurship interface

is direct and similar to the marketing/organisation interface of large firms. This theory-building research showed the marketing/entrepreneurship interface is more complex than the literature suggests and sets a foundation for further research about the interface'.

4 CONCLUSION

In summary, this chapter addressed the problem: *How should postgraduate research candidates and their supervisors present the thesis?* It argued that a thesis should follow certain style conventions and have five sections: introduction, literature review, methodology, analysis of data, and conclusions and implications.

In conclusion, a candidate has to master the skills required to present a thesis just as much as they have to master research techniques. A candidate who follows this structure will make their thesis match the expectations of most examiners and they will have been trained for later research work.

APPENDIX A—A RESEARCH PROPOSAL STRUCTURE KEYED TO THE THESIS STRUCTURE

At many universities, candidates in research programs are required to present a research proposal during or at the start of their candidature This appendix provides a suggested outline for a university's proposal that fits with the structured approach to presenting theses in Chapter 1 and incorporates my students' experiences and Poole (1993) and Krathowl (1977). Any research proposal should be carefully tailored to the organisation asking for it, so the format below should always be adjusted to suit other requirements.

The proposal is equivalent to Christopher Columbus asking the king and queen of Spain for some ships to sail west. He had to say convincingly how his voyage would increase knowledge of the world by building on existing knowledge to find a shorter route to the Orient; and why Spain should approve his request to set sail after his presentation.

As a rule of thumb, a research proposal should be about 20 to 30 pages in length (with the list of references and any appendices of support material being additional to this page count), but the estimates of word and page lengths given below are very tentative. The proposal could have about ten to twenty or so references. Remember to check spelling and to provide page numbers at the middle top of each page.

Incidentally, having read at least one or two completed proposals and one or two completed theses similar to the planned one, is a good inspiration and guide for the task ahead. As well, this appendix should be read in conjunction with the chapter above about how to present a thesis.

1 OBJECTIVES OF THE PROGRAM

To begin, discuss what the research project will be about.

1.1 Introduction and research problem

The introduction is a quarter to half page picture of the whole proposal, showing the major controversies or gaps in the literature that lead to the research problem. This description in the proposal may become Section 1.1 in the final thesis.

The research problem is presented at the end of this section, in italics and indented. Note that readers of a research proposal cannot be expected to know the jargon of every discipline, and so the title and research problem should be expressed in as simple terms as possible to suit the likely readers, and any specialist terms should be defined in this section as they are introduced.

1.2 Justification for the research

This section is about one page and justifies the research, usually on four dimensions:

- gaps in the literature (provide several references in support and refer to Section 3 below)
- size and complexity of the industry or processes involved
- unusual methodology to be used (provide several references in support and refer to Section 4 below)
- possible benefits of outcomes for policy and for practice.

This section of the proposal becomes Section 1.3 in the thesis.

2 RELATION TO PREVIOUS RESEARCH

The reader needs to be assured that the research project will produce a contribution.

2.1 Preliminary literature review and conceptual framework with its related research issues

In about two pages, show the major issues and schools in the parent theory literature and the gaps in the parent theory literature, and then *briefly* outline and justify a new conceptual framework and some related research issues/questions (for qualitative research) or propositions/hypotheses (for quantitative research) arising from the gaps that are planned to be the focus of data collection and data analysis—this conceptual framework and its related issues or propositions/hypotheses is the research problem theory described in the chapter above, of course. A model of the conceptual framework with circles and arrows would be impressive. The discussion of the parent theories becomes the first part of Chapter 2 in the thesis and the section about a conceptual framework and its related research issues becomes the later parts of Chapter 2. Define key terms as this section of the proposal progresses or have a definition sub-section.

The research setting could be briefly described here, too; see the discussion of this issue in this book's chapter above.

2.2 Contribution of the research

A contribution is a *change* to a body of knowledge created by a research project. This section complements and expands on Section 2 above about the justification for the research. This section describes the specific *outcomes* of the research to be developed in Chapter 5 of the thesis, and describes their importance. For example, it discusses the newness of the model that will be developed to fill the gaps in the body of knowledge noted in Section 1.2 above, or a checklist that will be developed for managers who have no guides at present. In brief, this section is specific about likely outcomes and their importance. A candidate could also mention a conference at which a paper about the research could be presented, such as the annual conference of the Australia and New Zealand Association for Management (ANZAM). As well, the title of a journal that might publish an article about the research could be mentioned.

2.3 Delimitations of scope with justifications

Outline and *justify* the major delimitations that will be placed on the research, for example, industry, level of management and states or country. No claim for generalisability will be made beyond these limits. This section could be kept to about one third of a page. This section in the proposal becomes Section 1.7 of the thesis.

3 RESEARCH METHODS AND PLAN

How will data be collected and analysed to produce the contributions above?

3.1 Methodology of data collection and analysis

This section about the planned steps to collect and analyse data would be about five to ten pages in length. It should be both comprehensive and concise, with references to support its judgements. Again, avoid jargon that non-specialists might not know, or explain or describe what is meant by specialist terms. Topics could include:

- justification of a quantitative or qualitative paradigm
- justification of the methodology within that paradigm (with preferably an explanation why some alternative methodologies were not used), using terms such as how many interviews and who they will be with, interview guides and especially the unit of analysis
- arrangements for access to the data, for example, agreements from people to be interviewed
- possible ways of analysing data, for example, the matrix method of analysing qualitative data suggested by Miles & Huberman (1994).

This section should have at least three references to textbooks or articles about methodology, to justify the proposed steps. Section 3.3 about Chapter 3 Methodology in the body of this chapter provides guidance about some details that could be covered here. As an indication of the details required, a proposal for a quantitative methodology should indicate the operational definitions of the constructs in the proposed propositions/hypotheses of Section 3 of this appendix (for example, how 'firm size' will be measured). In addition, scales and their accompanying statistical test should have been thought through (for example, a rank scale needs a nonparametric test). Tables of these considerations would be helpful.

This section in the proposal becomes Chapter 3 of the thesis.

4 THESIS OUTLINE AND TIMETABLE

Some final points need to be dealt with, to add credibility to the proposal.

4.1 Thesis outline
In the proposal, one or two lines describing each planned chapter in the thesis should suffice, especially if the standard five chapter structure will be used. This proposal section becomes Section 1.5 of the thesis.

4.2 Timetable
The timetable could be shown for each chapter. It is possible to plan the months and pages of a postgraduate research project. As a rough rule of thumb, the five chapters have these respective percentages of the thesis' words: 6, 34, 18, 22 and 20 percent. Using these approximate percentages, a candidate could plan the time and pages for any chapter, as shown in this chapter's Section 2.1 Perspectives on the overall structure. Note that Phillips and Pugh (2007, p. 88) have a timetable for a PhD program that is not very much different from Table 1. This section and the next ones are in the proposal only and are not in the completed thesis.

5 RESOURCES AND OTHER DETAILS

Finally, what will it cost the researcher's organisation?

5.1 Resource requirements
A tentative estimate of direct funding requirements might be useful, for example, postage for survey mailings, and who will pay for them. Justifications and sources of estimates are required for each expense item, for example, the date a quote was received from Qantas or a price list of a computer supplier. Printing costs of questionnaires will require estimates of their length and the price per page to print. There should be no surprises in the budget items, for they should flow naturally out of the earlier sections about the aims and design of the research. For example, car hire should not be just costed, but why car hire was necessary rather than public transport should be explained and its use related back to overall aims of the research.

This estimate in the proposal is not the formal request for the funding, and acceptance of the proposal does *not* mean funding has been approved. If outside funding is being used, make it clear that academic integrity will not be jeopardised by acceptance of that funding.

5.2 Background of the researcher
This is a brief section outlining any pilot studies that the researcher has done, and his or her research qualifications and experience, for example, titles, methodologies and word lengths of dissertations.

REFERENCES

Krathwohl, DR 1977, *How to Prepare a Research Proposal*, University of Syracuse.

Miles, MB & Huberman, AM 1994, *Qualitative Data Analysis*, Sage, New York.

Phillips, EM & Pugh, DS 2000, *How to Get a PhD*, 3rd edn, Open University Press, Milton Keynes.

Poole, ME 1993, 'Reviewing for research excellence: expectations, procedures and outcomes', *Australian Journal of Education*, vol. 37, no. 3, pp. 219-230.

APPENDIX B—TYPES OF QUESTIONS AN EXAMINER MIGHT ASK THEMSELF

These are questions that reviewers of two journals have been told to consider in their review of a submitted article. They show the types of questions that a thesis examiner might ask as they go through your thesis. The sources are from the editor of Journal of Service Management (Johnston, R 1996, 'How to get published', mimeo) and Personnel Review (extracted from a reviewer's report about an article I submitted to that journal in 2010).

abstract — includes findings?
intro — signposts of journey, objectives, underlying idea?
lit. review — knowledge of, use of, up-to-date?
model — flows from lit., sensible, useful?
data — instrument, methods, summary of results?
discussion — related to model?
conclusion/implications — what's the contribution? so what? what next?
references — style, all there?

Originality:
Does the paper contain new and significant information adequate to justify publication: Theory? New data? Analysis? Results? Application of theory to practice? Summarizing the state of knowledge? Methodology?

Relationship to Literature:
Does the paper demonstrate an adequate understanding of the relevant literature in the field and cite an appropriate range of literature sources? Is any significant work ignored? Is adequate credit given to other contributors in the field? Are there major omissions? Are the references complete?

Methodology:
Is the paper's argument built on an appropriate base of theory, concepts, or other ideas? Has the research or equivalent intellectual work on which the paper is based been well designed? Are the methods employed appropriate?

Results:
Are results presented clearly and analysed appropriately? Do the conclusions adequately tie together the other elements of the paper?

Implications for research, practice and/or society:
Does the paper identify clearly any implications for research, practice and/or society? Does the paper bridge the gap between theory and practice? How can the research be used in practice (economic and commercial impact), in teaching, to influence public policy, in research (contributing to the body of knowledge)? What is the impact upon society (influencing public attitudes, affecting quality of life)? Are these implications consistent with the findings and conclusions of the paper?

Quality of communication:
Does the paper clearly express its case, measured against the technical language of the field and the expected knowledge of the journal's readership? Has attention been paid to the clarity of expression and readability, such as sentence structure, jargon use, acronyms, etc.

ACKNOWLEDGEMENTS

These notes were originally based on ideas of Drs Geoff Meredith, Bert Cunnington and Mike Watkins and also on University of Oregon (n.d.). However, views and errors are the writer's own. He has written this chapter with a beginning postgraduate research candidate in mind, and so has presented some positions as starting points for drafting a thesis rather than as the only positions that can be adopted.

He thanks Drs Kwaku Atuahene-Gima, Robert Brown, Alan Buttery, Gail Craswell, Hank Johnson, Di Lewis, Estelle Phillips, John Roberts and John Rossiter, Barry Bell, Diana Best, Claudia Hope and Tony Ward for commenting on earlier drafts, and thanks Barry Bell, Len Coote, June Dunleavy, Marilyn Healy, John Jackson, Ben Lyttle, Cec Pederson, Tony Ward and Vicky Schinkel for ideas for some examples. I sincerely thank them all.

A slightly shortened and early version of this chapter has been published as Perry, C 1998a, 'A structured approach for presenting theses', *Australasian Marketing Journal*, vol. 6, no.1, pp. 63-85. An article about its usefulness in doctoral programs is Perry (2011). Writing a thesis should be based on examples/exemplars, just as writing an article is (as explained in Chapter 2 of this book). Examples on the Internet of theses that used this approach are:

- Rao, S 2003, The impact of internet use on inter-firm relationships in service industries, PhD thesis, Griffith University, Brisbane.

Available from Australian Digital Theses at http://www.griffith.edu.au/ins/collections/adt/

- Stokes, R 2004, Inter-organisational relationships for events tourism strategy making in Australian states and territories, PhD thesis, Griffith University, Brisbane. Available from www.scholar.google.com.

CHAPTER 2

COMPREHENSIVE PROCESSES OF EFFICIENT ARTICLE WRITING

ABSTRACT

Writing journal articles is an essential skill for an academic. This book chapter introduces the core principles of that skill, based on the literature. The chapter's theme is that article writing is a collaborative craft and not a mysterious art—it is the craft of conversation. Writing the first draft of an article may take two or so days; however, writing a draft table of contents, planning and collecting data with colleagues beforehand, and then re-drafting that first draft many times and revising it after the reviewers have looked at it, will take many months. Then the joy of acceptance into a conversation will probably come. The chapter covers four segments: targeting an article's readers; getting read and cited; the structure and style of writing an article; and redrafting, sending off and revising.

For acknowledgements and thanks, please refer to the end of this chapter.

INTRODUCTION

Publishing articles in peer-reviewed journals is an essential skill for a modern academic. Your articles will advance knowledge about the discipline you love and will let you join conversations with people from around the world who share your interests—you will no longer just listen to others from the sidelines. As well, articles will advance your career and raise the reputation of your university or research institution (and hence raise your reputation). However, getting published in journals is becoming harder (Varadarajan 1996) as all universities around the world set higher standards for promotion and so urge staff to publish more.

Thus this book chapter aims to establish a modern starting point for writers of articles—it updates and broadens the reach of the literature about efficient article writing by looking in practical detail at the wide range of processes involved, in this one chapter. Essentially, I argue that article writing is a collaborative *craft* and not a mysterious art—it is the craft of *conversation* (Huff 1999). Writing the first draft of an article may take two or so days (Day 1996; Perry 1997). However, all the other steps involved will take many months, including planning and collecting data with colleagues beforehand, refining that first draft many times, and revising it after editors and reviewers have looked at it. Then the joy of acceptance into a conversation will probably come. In more detail, the steps are:

1. Start with a team planning synopsis with its target journal and a structure/table of contents; the structure/table of contents in that synopsis should cover three numbered levels of sections.
2. To facilitate citation of an article, have an appropriate title, abstract and introduction.
3. Set a deadline of two equivalent days to write the first draft.
4. Revise the draft many times after others have reviewed them, then submit the article and happily revise it for reviewers (or, revise, recast, update and try a backup journal if it is rejected).

These steps apply to both quantitative and qualitative research reports in most academic journals. The steps are synthesised from literature about writing (like Armstrong 1997; Belcher 2009a; Bem 2002; Day 2007, Huff 1999; Jonnson 2006; Murray 2009; Rocco & Hatcher 2011; Stewart 2002; Summers 2002), including my own articles about writing (Carson, Gilmore, Perry & Gronhaug 2001; Gilmore, Carson & Perry 2006; Perry 1997; Perry, Carson & Gilmore 2003). That is, the steps are not based solely on my own experience.

Many aspects of how to write an article are covered in detail in this book's Chapter 1 about thesis writing. For example, how to write a literature review and how to analyse data are dealt with in depth in this book's Chapter 1. Indeed, writing a thesis following this book's Chapter 1 is closely allied with writing a journal article, as shown in Exhibit 1 (Perry 2011, p. 3).

This chapter has four parts. The first is about targeting an article's readers. The next is about getting the article read and cited. Then aspects of writing like structure and style are covered. The final part is about redrafting, sending off and revising.

Exhibit 1 — How writing an article aligns with writing the sections of a thesis

THESIS	ARTICLE
parent theories 1 and 2 in Chapter 2	paragraphs 2 and 3
justification in Section 1.3	paragraph 4
research problem theory of Section 2.3	Literature review section
methodology of Chapter 3	Methodology section
data analysis of Chapter 4	Findings section
conclusions in Sections 5.2 and 5.3	Discussion section
implications of Sections 5. 4 and 5.5	Implications section

Source: *based on Perry (2011, p. 3)*

TARGETING AN ARTICLE'S READERS

The basic principle behind publishing an article is to *contribute to a conversation*. That is, the core of an article is an idea that intrigues you and should interest someone else. That idea may initially pop up during discussions with colleagues at a conference or over a cup of coffee at work, while answering a question by a student, while reading an article or in the further research section of your thesis (and they may pop up at the gym or swimming pool, too (Day 1997)). Thus, to keep up with cutting edge ideas in your field, grasp chances for one-on-one talks with experienced experts in your field at conferences or when they visit your university; and volunteer to review articles in your field for conferences and even for journals (Appendix A of this book's Chapter 1; Summers 2002, p. 414). The initial idea for an article is often at the intersection of two 'parent theories' as shown in this book's Chapter 1 about thesis writing. These fields are parent theories like eco-tourism and relationship marketing that have tracks about them at conferences, or have a journal dedicated to them; the fields could include one or two methodologies. To verify that such a gap exists, put two keywords about the parent theories into an electronic library database like ABI/Inform to confirm that little has been written about their intersection.

Because the time between having the original idea and its eventual publication takes months or years, an academic needs to have a portfolio of articles-in-progress. The articles should be positioned in just one or two fields where you want to establish yourself over the next five or so years. Specialising in one or two fields is necessary to get any sort of track record, because getting to know a field sufficiently well to publish within it takes so long. Thus, the portfolio is a long term, sequenced, rolling, planned program of articles in those fields.

The five or so-year portfolio can be written on a whiteboard in your office if you are an extrovert, or on a piece of paper that is on the top of the top drawer of your desk. It is regularly updated because the portfolio will have rows for each article-in-progress and seven columns for:

1. the article-in-progress's topic
2. the target journal (and possibly the backup journal if the target journal rejects)
3. the co-authors
4. planned month/year of initial submission to the journal
5. the current stage
6. the estimated month/year of the end of this current stage
7. comments on article-in-progress such as a planned conference about it.

(The current stage in column 5 could have codes for each stage. For example, the code of 1 could stand for selecting the journal and its two exemplar articles, 2 for the structure/table of contents, 3 for studying the literature and clarifying the gap, 4 for data collection, 5 for data analysis, 6 for writing the '2-day' first draft, 7 for later drafts, 8 for others' reviews, 9 for submit, 10 for revise....)

After establishing the month/year details in your portfolio, be more specific and detailed in your *daily/weekly schedules*. For example, ensure you have set aside 2 to 5 hours per week in semester time for writing in a quiet space (Belcher 2009a; Murray 2009) such as your office at home, or your office at work (with the door locked and no doorknocks answered). These planned hours should be in blocks lasting at least 2 hours ('Writing an article' n.d.), but grab any shorter, unplanned blocks of time to keep working on an article, if the time becomes available because of cancelled meetings, for example. In other words, article writing consists of both short snacks and lengthy meals (Murray 2009).

Conferences are a key to all this conversation-joining. Target three or more years of the same annual conference *in a row* to develop a relationship with others that could eventually flower into co-authorships, and target all the sessions at each conference in just one or two *tracks*—your aim is to meet others in the track audience who are interested in your topic just as much as it is to meet the presenters of a particular paper. Arrange to meet informally with key people (even beforehand), go regularly to all Meet the Editors sessions, and talk with the editors about the suitability of a possible article for their journal. Practice the '30 second elevator summary' of your research for informal occasions and meetings, and take lots of your business cards. Thank anyone who has helped you afterwards by email, with hopes (but not firm plans) for the next conference. Set up 'karma' by giving to others before you expect to receive anything from them, for example, send them an article or a bibliography even if they have not sent you anything. Very importantly, before the conference, know the specific journal where you will publish your conference paper afterwards (Murray 2009). Finally, join informal discussions about how professional or horrid some journal editors and their reviewers (and PhD examiners) can be.

By the way, presenting a paper at a conference requires skills. Know how many minutes are available and rehearse the presentation before the session. Start with some ideas that are focussed on the audience's concerns. Present the key, interesting ideas and not the whole paper—anyone interested in the whole paper can read it in the proceedings. Make eye contact with the audience—do not read the paper. Have no more than one PowerPoint slide per minute. On each slide, have no more than seven lines with no more than seven words per line; and insert slide numbers that the audience can refer to when they raise comments or questions in the time at the end of the presentation. In that time for comments and questions, do not hog the time for your own explanations or be too defensive—ask the questioners to expand on their views and acknowledge how their comments will be considered. After your presentation, go outside for some minutes while you write down issues that the audience raised, to incorporate into the subsequent journal article (Murray 2009). Opt for publication of only a short version or abstract of your paper in the proceedings if the conference allows it, because many journals do not accept articles that have been published as a paper in the proceedings. Some other journals do accept articles based on conference papers, but first check with the editor by email whether the journal accepts *revised* conference papers (that is, assure the editor it has been revised since it was a mere conference paper).

The background behind the writing of an article has been established above. The next step is to identify the target journal, for each journal is different from other journals, just as its readers are different from other academics, researchers and research students. About half of submissions are rejected because they were sent to the wrong journal:

> the most common cause of outright rejection before entering the review process is that the paper is not suited to the journal ... On average, about half of all submissions are rejected ... I found consistent agreement amongst readers, authors, editors and reviewers: How people view each journal *is unique per journal, but common within its readership*. (Day 1996, italics added)

This identification of one target journal from among about three or four possibilities takes three hours or so of Internet search time. An author needs to know a possible target journal's editorial objectives, its notes for authors, the table of contents for four or so past issues, plus any editor's comments in the first and last issues of this year, or when a new editor takes over. To demonstrate that the journal has actually been targeted as the editor hopes it has been, an author should:

- Include one or two appropriate, core words from the editorial objectives into the abstract and the first paragraph of the article (Jonnson 2006).
- Carefully read the journal's exemplar articles discussed in the paragraph below.
- Cite and reference at least three or four *relevant articles* from *recent* issues of the target journal (including those by the editor or members the editorial board)—if you cannot find these relevant articles in the target journal, perhaps you are targeting the wrong journal.
- Keep to the word limits of the journal's articles and abstracts.

The first target journal is usually the highest ranking one that could reasonably be expected to accept the article. Search Google for the rankings of journal in your field. Business journal rankings are at <http://www.abdc.edu.au/3.43.0.0.1.0.htm> for the authoritative Australian Business Deans' Council journal ratings; and at <www.harzing.com> for 18 different sets of rankings.

Next, look at three or so exemplar articles from the target journal that show how the journal's articles are presented. An exemplar shows 'how' to write the article and not 'what' to write (Huff 1999). Some exemplars may not have used your methodology, but at least one should have used your methodology like case research or action research. For example, the exemplars show:

- the upper and lower limits of words and paragraphs in the introduction section and the literature review section
- how the importance of the gap can be described
- how the methodology is reported
- how further research is presented before or after the implications
- if the conclusion has its own section heading
- how many references are listed
- how figures and graphs are presented
- the structure and number of words in the article and the abstract.

I know two very well-published, full Professors who look in any target journal for recent articles by one or two eminent authors whom they admire, and then use those authors' articles as exemplars for that journal.

Now consider co-authors. Having a small stable of long-term co-authors who write several articles together is important. Each co-author brings something to the table, that is, each should have a team role like methodology, literature review or writing coordination. Establish a team culture with each stable of co-authors, for example, the culture could cover points like: that meetings start on time, that first names are used, the number of days that a draft sits on each co-author's desk before they pass it back, how Microsoft Office 365 or Google Drive is used, and how milestones like acceptance are celebrated (Rocco & Hatcher 2011).

Establishing these stables of co-authors is a key to academic progress. The first co-author will usually be a doctoral supervisor (so having a well-published author as a supervisor is important). That first co-author should be a guide to other mentors in your field(s) about how to write, where to publish, joining networks of people with similar interests, and conferences. Then you yourself will find other mentors and/or co-authors at conferences or when they visit a university (so talking to visitors and to many people at the one or two tracks you attend in three or more annual conferences in a row is important). The first step in approaching a possible co-author is to know something about what they have written and tell them how interesting it was. Then tell them about your own interests. Then tell them about a possible joint article for which you already have some strengths, but for which you need a co-author to help handle aspects like methodology or background literature. To demonstrate that you do indeed have something to add to the potential partnership, the team planning synopsis described in the next paragraph could be useful, as could a draft structure/table of contents of the article described in a later section. (I once wrongly showed a draft of a complete article to someone I was hoping to work with, rather than the structure/table of contents, and he said that he could not improve the draft. So we never wrote anything together.)

A team planning synopsis (Day 2007, p. 88) can be a useful starting point for an agenda for the first meeting with co-authors about a joint article (the meeting can be done online). The synopsis covers eight points:

1 early ideas about the target readership like marketing researchers, for example. If possible, some of the target readers should be 'three or four real-life people' (Brown 1996)
2 the target journal
3 the article's aims, for example, what gap it will address
4 benefits to readers and implications for their practice
5 an outline of the paper's structure/table of contents
6 the article's length
7 when it will be ready and
8 details and team roles of the co-authors (with a possible order of the list of authors). Whenever I write out the agenda for the meeting about the team planning synopsis, I hope to be the first co-author.

All team members should know the Vancouver Protocol about authorship ('What rules determine authorship on publications?' 2011, p. 1) (as should all supervisors and their research students). The Protocol says all team members must contribute in all three ways to avoid charges of academic misconduct—authorship is 'a substantial contribution in **all three** of:

1. conception and design, **or** analysis and interpretation of data;
2. drafting the article **or** revising it critically for important intellectual content; and
3. final approval of the version to be published.'

Some team members have been too busy to send me their approval of the final version required in the third way above, so I now email the final version to members and say something like, 'If I do not hear from you by 5 pm next Friday 12 October, I will assume you approve it'. If a team member does not meet these three criteria, they should not be listed as a co-author but should be thanked in the Acknowledgements section of the article.

So the gap has been identified, the first target journal decided, exemplar articles found and the team established. Now the article can be written; the rest of this chapter is about that article writing.

GETTING READ AND CITED

We write an article so that it can be cited in other articles. If other authors cite us, it means we have actually joined into a conversation with them. Getting cited means others have actually heard what we have said, and so our number of citations is a measure of how much we have influenced others. However, getting cited is not easy, for most articles are never cited and about one quarter of those that are cited are cited only once (Brown 1996). That is, the writers of most articles have probably wasted their time! However, you can increase the chances of your article being read and cited by others by making the article 'sticky' enough for potential readers to stop to read your article before they continue their rush through the lists of hundreds in an electronic library database like Google Scholar.

By the way, you can find your own personal citation count from <www.harzing.com/pop.htm>. Download the program to your desktop and then put in your name (or someone else's name), the years you are interested in, un-tick all fields except 'Business...' and 'Arts...', say, and then click on 'Lookup'. Then un-tick any article that is not one of yours. Now you can see your own citation count.

Potential readers will start their search of a library **database** with keywords. So have as many keywords as the journal will allow, and make them attractive to the interests of all the academics and research students who you want to cite you. For example, deciding whether to use any or all of the keywords of 'Generations', 'Generation X', 'Generation Y' and 'Baby boomers' will require careful thought about likely readers.

Next, potential readers will look at the **title**. Essentially, the title should summarise the key message of an article. The title should be as long as the journal allows so that some sticky words are in there; having a colon in the middle will help achieve this goal. (But titles more than 10 words long are hard to remember and are less likely to be downloaded.) Sometimes the title could be a snappy and informative sentence about the topic and findings, and have some of the attractive keywords in it, for example, 'Decision analysis helps wheat agribusiness management' (Brown, Rogers & Pressland 1994). Be warned that reviewers and editors of serious journals do not want smart-alecky, too-clever-by-half titles in their serious journal. So look at titles of articles in the journal to see how they are written and which ones stand out to you.

If your keywords and title are sticky enough, potential readers will then look at your **abstract**. Know the word limit for the target journal's abstracts, and then try to fit as many of these points into your abstract as you can (based on Brown, Rogers & Pressland 1994):

1. a short, topical theme sentence about the general field to orientate the reader
2. the aim
3. why the research was done, that is, what is the gap and why is it important?
4. the contribution of the article (related to the gap, of course)
5. how the data was collected and analysed, that is, the methodology
6. what were the results/findings, that is, the patterns in the data
7. the implications for policy and practice (details about them, not waffle).

Note: include some distinctive words from the journal's editorial objectives into the abstract and into the first paragraph, to catch the editor's eye. As usual, look at exemplar articles to see how each journal likes abstracts to be written; for example, some journals prefer the aim in the abstract in the form of 'Examines …' rather than 'This article examines …'

Here is an abstract that has six of the seven points above; the only point it misses is the explicit description of the contribution:

> Taiwan has been targeted as one Asian market with the potential to supply large numbers of tourists to Australia, however, the market has eased after a promising start in the early 1990s. This paper examines the role of material culture in determining visitor satisfaction among Taiwanese tourists. [Is this the literature's gap/contribution?]. One hundred and fifty Taiwanese tourists travelling on inclusive tours were surveyed in South East Queensland. The major findings were that most Taiwanese respondents believed that culture did not play a major role in determining their satisfaction levels and they expressed a high level of satisfaction with their visit. The implications of these findings are that although Taiwanese culture is important to the Taiwanese visitor in a holiday destination, they are tolerant of cross-cultural differences and therefore do not evaluate their vacation based on these differences. (Master & Prideaux 1998, p. 445)

If the abstract is sticky enough, a potential reader next looks at the **Introduction**. This beginning should cite many articles about the field—you start to join a conversation by showing you have listened to previous speakers. In brief, the introduction is an executive summary to give the potential reader an enticing glimpse of what is to come, and is not a 'whodunit?' (Day 1996). In effect, the Introduction section is a quick drive around the streets of a town that will be walked through in the more detailed Literature review section.

Any introduction should have five core points in its paragraphs (based on Swales 1984):

1.1 Establish the background field, assert its significant position in theory and practice.
1.2 Summarise previous research (only one or two paragraphs, enough to prove there is an important gap in step 3 below).
1.3 Indicate gaps, inconsistencies and/or controversies, and why it is important that researchers should address them; this importance is becoming a more critical consideration in a modern editor's acceptance of an article, so write at least one paragraph about this. How to show this importance is discussed later in this book chapter.
1.4 State the aim or purpose of present research (to address point 3) and state briefly the position that your article will establish about the aim. Then write at least one sentence that states explicitly what your 'contribution' is (related to point 1.3)—this is what the editor and potential readers are most interested in.
1.5 Provide a brief outline of the sections of the article.

Articles by eminent writers in A or A* journals will usually cover these five points.

The contribution and its importance are critical to an article's acceptance by a journal. The contribution can *build* theory, or build and *test* theory. Some journals accept articles that just build theory. That is, a contribution can be just the development of a *conceptual framework* that brings together previously separate fields (like parent theories were brought together in theses in this book's Chapter 1) or explains previously confused understandings (by expanding current interpretations or adding new variables to previous understandings, for example). Some journals publish non-empirical articles that review how the literature in a field is unclear and suggest frameworks for future researchers (Webster & Watson 2002;

Taylor n.d.). These articles have all the parts of the articles described in this book chapter except for the methodology and data analysis parts. However, a new framework has to be developed in both a theory building article, and in a more 'empirical' article that builds and tests a theory by including a description of the collection and analysis of data about the theory. Thus empirical articles that both build and test a theory will probably be more acceptable to more journals than theory building/literature review articles. So this chapter will focus on the more common empirical articles.

How 'big' should a *contribution* be? The answer is: as big as necessary to be accepted by the target journal. So go for a big contribution if you are targeting a high-reputation journal. As the editor of such a journal explains, quality is more important than quantity:

> Often, a single paper using all the available data makes for a far stronger contribution than several papers each with a far more modest contribution. Therefore, even when the first study is published, the second study may not be. The result is a weaker first paper and no second paper. (Stewart 2002, p. 4).

That is, one big contribution article will do more for your reputation in the long run than several articles with smaller contributions (Huff 1999). Several issues can be raised to show how important is the contribution, from this book's Chapter 1:

    i the research outcomes will be innovative and novel by describing the relative neglect of the specific research problem by previous researchers—this research will advance the knowledge base of the discipline
    ii the importance and complexity of the industry and/or the importance of the specific area being investigated like parts of a supply chain or of a management process (this justification is usually accompanied by a mass of statistical data showing how huge the area of the research problem is in terms of constructs such as revenue, employment and assets, and is sometimes accompanied by authoritative discussions and quotations from government publications about committees of inquiry), to show how the research might result in national economic, environment and/or social benefits
    iii the relative neglect of the research's methodologies by previous researchers
    iv the usefulness of potential applications of the research's findings to organisations and other relevant end-users.

Note that top journals usually look for universal, not just local, contributions because findings within a small, local context will interest only locals, and may be the same as the findings in other contexts—'Just because a particular phenomenon has not been studied in a particular context (such as a specific industry or country) is not a good reason to do a study' (Stewart 2002, p. 4). So local context research should have distinctive justifications like a context's culture or economy that is different from those of other, already researched contexts, and these differences explain why new findings could be different from more universal findings. That is, the study should have implications for our understanding of the distinctive features of the context like culture or economy.

Before finally reading the whole article, a potential reader who has stuck with you so far, is likely to go directly to the **Conclusion**. A conclusion should have no new material because the conclusion merely ties together what has already been discussed. It should summarise what has been said, and emphasise the contributions. Then it integrates the whole article by briefly repeating what is the solution to the aim of the article that was outlined in the introduction. Thus I now start the two paragraphs in the conclusion section of my articles with these two phrases: 6.1 'In summary, …' and 6.2 'In conclusion, …'

After a potential reader has stuck with you through the keywords, the abstract, the introduction and the conclusion, they will hopefully read your article and cite it. But there are additional ways of increasing the chances of being cited:

- Cite many other, relevant writers, to set up the karma for them to cite you.
- Possibly set up a 'citation club' whose members commit to citing each other's articles (such arrangements seem somewhat shady to me).
- Research 'hot' topics in your area so that many researchers will come across your articles.
- Put your articles on your own and/or your university's or a listserv's web site (check with the journal editor first), to make them easier to get hold of.
- Join Internet discussion groups like methodspace.com and make comments about your own articles there.
- Build networks with other writers in your field at conferences and during their university visits (including journal editors), so that they will search for your name in library databases.

WRITING - STRUCTURE, STYLE

All the items in the section above about citations do not need to be written in the order above, because we have to get to the first draft of the body of the article soon. But a key point needs to be made before we do that writing. The first draft is *not* written first—the structure/table of contents of the whole article has to be written *before* the first draft of the article is written. Only then is the first draft written. That draft need not be actually written in the order of the structure/table of contents, but it should be written to a self-imposed timetable—blocks of hours up to the equivalent of two full days should finish this first draft. (Some inexperienced writers may like to write a first draft before they consider a detailed structure/table of contents. But the processes recommended in this book chapter are those that have actually been found to assist *efficient*, productive and professional writers (Ehrenreich 2001, p. 17; Huff 1999, p. 78; Murray 2002, pp. 105-7, 231-31; Phillips & Pugh 2000, pp. 67-70; Zuber-Skerritt & Knight 1992, pp. 200-201). One writing workshop facilitator says to writers who cannot construct an initial structure/table of contents to three levels of detail, that they should construct it to just one or two levels of detail and then write the first draft. After that draft, they extract a more detailed structure/table of contents from the draft, and make sure the text conforms to that detailed structure in the later drafts (Rob Brown 2012, pers. comm., 7 December).)

So consider that **structure/table of contents** in detail. That structure/table of contents is established down to three levels of detail. The structure is not set in stone for it can be altered as writing proceeds. But it is important, as established in the paragraph above. If possible, in the structure, follow the pattern expected by the reader. That is, an article should have six sections/headings: (1) an introduction, (2) a review of the extant literature review ending in research issues or hypotheses about the gaps in the literature, (3) methodology, (4) results/findings, (5) discussion and (6) conclusion. Use numbers for each heading down to two decimal place levels for planning purposes, even if the journal does not, for example, '2 Literature review', '2.1 Marketing to different generations', '2.2.1 Marketing to generation Y'. Then put the *number of words* in each of the first or second level sections on to each in your numbered list of the initial structure/table of contents (Murray 2009). Doing all this initial, detailed planning helps to make the article more coherent and less repetitive, and plants the seeds in your unconscious that will flower when you are writing the later first draft of the article. By the way, the headings of the sections should be descriptive, that is, longer than two words, to show the new direction in which the article is going.

Consider the major parts of an article in that list of numbered sections in the structure/table of contents in more detail (see this book's Chapter 1; Gilmore, Carson & Perry 2005). The article has an hour glass shape (Bem 2002). It starts broad with other, previous research reported in the literature; then it narrows to the one research project being reported in the article; and then it broadens again with implications for other people like scholars, managers and policy makers, and other researchers. That is, after the introduction described above, the **literature review** covers the ideas in the extant literature around the topic. Write about themes/ideas, not about authors. After all, the reviewer will be familiar with most of the literature. Thus, the start of a paragraph should be a theme/topic sentence in the writer's *own* words and ideas that summarises what the writer will argue for in the paragraph. That is, the paragraph should not begin with 'Smith (2000) said...', for example (of course, Smith must still be cited in brackets at the end of any sentence). Taylor (n.d., p. 1) summarises this advice about the first sentence in a paragraph and the reason for it:

> It's usually a bad sign to see every paragraph beginning with the name of a researcher. Instead, organize the literature review into sections that present themes or identify trends, including relevant theory. You are not trying to list all the material published, but to synthesize and evaluate it according to the guiding concept of your thesis or research question.

Indeed, an author's name should usually be inside brackets in *all* the sentences in a paragraph (Bem 2002). Putting authors' names inside brackets forces you to explain your *own* line of argument, rather than freeloading off the ideas of others. Keeping quotations to a minimum helps in this regard, too.

As well, all literature reviews should finish at the 'destination' of all literature reviews: a new conceptual framework with its justified hypotheses/research questions about gaps in the background literature, to guide future research (Webster & Watson 2002). The whole literature review is written with that final conceptual framework in mind—'your task is to cut and polish it, to select the facets to highlight, and to craft the best setting for it' (Bem 2002, p. 3).

The next major section is about the methodology used to collect and analyse data about the hypotheses/research questions uncovered in the literature review section. (How to write this section and the following sections, is described in this book's Chapter 1). The methodology section includes justification of the methods used, how data was collected and analysed, and ethics. Next, the analysis of data or findings section uncovers patterns in the data about the hypotheses/research questions. In turn, the discussion section covers five points—it:

- demonstrates how contributions have been made to the extant literature by relating the findings back to the literature with verbs like, 'complement', 'extend', 'expand', 'add', 'enrich', 'build on' and 'explain'
- describes implications for the background theories/literature, for scholars
- outlines implications for managers/practitioners and for government and organizational policy makers
- acknowledges aspects of the study that could limit its internal and external validity, without giving so much detail about them that the research appears to have been a house of cards built on shaky foundations
- suggests directions for further research by researchers, and these could include ways of overcoming the limitations above.

Finally, the **conclusion** has the two points described above; that is, it has two paragraphs that could begin with 'In summary, …' and 'In conclusion, …'.

It is only *after* this structure is established down to three levels of detail, that the **first draft** is written quickly, say within two days equivalent, as noted. Follow the usual rules of style that were covered in the thesis writing in this book's Chapter 1, such as briefly describing the argument or point to be made in a section or paragraph in a theme/topic sentence at its beginning, for example, 'Seven deficiencies in models in the literature will be identified'. And make each step in the theme/topic easy to identify with or the judicious use of linkers such as 'firstly', 'secondly', or 'moreover', 'in addition', 'in contrast' and so on. (Handy lists of such linkers are at 'The writer's handbook using transitions' 2012). Other example rules of style are to use past and present tenses appropriately, and to put authors' names inside brackets (as discussed above). Citations and references have to be done exactly as they are described in the journal's notes for authors; and headings, and titles of figures and tables, have to be presented exactly as they are in the exemplars. Note that the reviewers should not be able to guess the author's name or affiliation (Peters & Cecci 1982), so do not cite and reference your own publications too much (self-citations do not count as citations after all), and never cite and reference your PhD (because few people read a PhD thesis—a thesis' good ideas should have been incorporated into journal articles).

REDRAFTING, SENDING OFF AND REVISING

After the first draft is written, the next drafts can be written. There are four increasingly 'nitty picky' drafting stages, with some days between each of them (Zuber-Skerritt & Knight 1992; Kallestinova 2011). The progression through them is how a writer gradually and properly moves from the creative, right side of the brain to the pedantic, left side of the brain. The four drafting stages after the initial structure/table of contents are:

0. Develop the structure/table of contents down to three levels of headings such as 2,2.1, and 2.1.1.
1. Get the first draft written quickly, within about two days equivalent, say (Day 1996). Do not get bogged down in too much pedantic detail in this draft—type'??' to indicate the uncertain spots that will have to be considered when the first draft is being revised.
2. Rearrange those first draft *ideas* in the second draft, for example, 'cut and paste' paragraphs and sentences.
3. Next, consider *words*. Check general spelling and grammar with the spellchecker; and remove section numbers and some headings of sections that are left over from the initial structure/table of contents.
4. Finally, check the journal's own style requirements like citations, references and headings (this is a very painful stage without Microsoft Endnote).

Removing the initial, temporary headings that were in the structure/table of contents from the third draft is a reminder that headings are merely supplementary and not critical to understanding an article—a reader should be able to follow the article without looking at any headings. That is, the first sentence after any heading should say what the heading has said but in slightly different words.

All this re-drafting needs to be done after earlier drafts have been reviewed by co-authors and other colleagues. Confirming this point, one journal editor has said: 'As an editor, I could usually identify the papers that had been read by no one other than the author before submission. Feedback helps and raises the odds of publication' (Stewart 2002, p. 5). Note how the acknowledgements section of key articles in your field usually has a long list of people who have read earlier drafts. But I wonder how these other people found the time to help the author re-draft the article? I suppose they had a reciprocal arrangement with the author—'I'll review your drafts if you will review mine'. Or the colleagues may have used the checklists in Appendix C of Huff (1999) that require merely a tick on a five-point scale for items for qualitative, quantitative, theory development and case study articles.

After all this re-drafting, the article can be submitted to the editor of the target journal. By this stage, the article should be as polished as possible because sending it off 'just to see comments' of reviewers about an unpolished draft will diminish your reputation with the editor (Huff 1999, p. 121). Nowadays, submission of an article is done electronically; note how the authors' names are kept separate from the article so the editor can send the article out to reviewers for anonymous review. Often the submission format allows the author an option to add extra comments for the editor. Grasp this opportunity to write a *very short* covering note that has the editor's name ('Dear Professor ...'), how the article addresses some of the editorial objectives of the journal, the article's contribution, and possiblty the number of the previous articles in the journal that you cite in the article—just in case the editor does not notice how appropriate the article is when they look at the submission.

Allow 8 to 12 weeks before checking on progress of an article (or about 2 to 4 weeks if no acknowledgment of submission is received, although online submissions are usually acknowledged straightaway). An editor is a busy person (Day n.d.; Gilmore, Carson & Perry 2006). They have many tasks: they have to find appropriate reviewers for the hordes of submissions that appear in their in-tray; track progress of each article; arbitrate between the conflicting reviewer's reports so that reviewers think their views have weight in the editor's decision-making; make a decision for authors about an article's acceptance, revision or rejection; encourage all promising authors to keep submitting articles to the journal into the future, whatever that decision; and frequently look at the citation rates or impacts of the journal to see if their editor's job is at risk. So an author should do what they can to ease the editor's load: know the latest editor's name and address, acknowledge everything promptly, respond with corrections within about a month if possible, supply the article precisely to specification after final acceptance, and do not amend proofs other than printer errors. Then the editor will look forward to your next submission. In other words, article writing needs a long term relationship with editors of journals, as well as long term relationships with co-authors, colleagues who reciprocally review drafts, and friends in audiences at conferences.

When an article is submitted, an editor will first check that the article is an appropriate one for their journal (about half of submissions are rejected at this stage, as noted above (Day n.d.)), and then select the reviewers if it is appropriate. This reviewer selection is sometimes based on the editor already having a rough idea about what a reviewer will say about an article, from their previous reviews. So if the article looks amateurish, it might be sent to a reviewer in the editor's stable of reviewers who is frequently harsh and will almost certainly reject it—a 'Dr No' reviewer. In contrast, an article by an author who has built a reputation with the editor for careful and thoughtful submissions, may be sent to a kinder reviewer. So always be polite with editors when writing messages to them and do whatever they want you to do (as well as meeting them at conferences). For example, why not email an editor a *short* 'thank you' message after your article has been accepted, or after they have spent time explaining why they have rejected an article?

The reviewers will judge an article using the journal's own set of criteria (see Chapter 1 Appendix B). There are four main criteria:

- Does it meet editorial objectives?
- What is the article's *contribution* to the fields that the journal's readers are interested in? How is the article demonstrably related to previous work in that field? Are the arguments employed valid in terms of that body of knowledge?
- Was the methodology handled well?
- Is the article easy to read? Do the arguments flow easily? Are the conclusions and implications strong?

The editor will synthesise the reviewers' judgements and make a decision. If the decision is **acceptance**, congratulations! More usually, the decision is **revision**, especially if the journal has expert reviewers who can provide constructive ideas about improvement. By the way, only one round of revisions before acceptance or rejection is becoming more common as journals become overwhelmed with submissions, but some journals still have two rounds of revisions before acceptance or rejection. Every author almost always becomes disappointed or angry when they read the editor's message about having to do revisions. So I suggest that you put the reviewer's report in a drawer for at least one week, and cool down. Then incorporate the reviewer's ideas with glee—this lovely person has raised your chances of acceptance from about less than 25% to more than 50% after the first review round and to more than 90% after the second review round (Stewart 2002). That is, do not pick up your bat and walk off the field like a spoilt brat if asked to revise. Do the revisions quickly, usually within a month—contributions can fade with time. Tell (and thank) the editor of your expected re-submission date if it is more than a week or so away (and tell them if you delay it). After you have done the revisions, review the article in its new totality for continuity and direction, for example, check the abstract and conclusion. Ask your review colleagues for their views. Then write a polite covering letter for each reviewer in turn, thanking them and saying how you addressed all their *numbered* suggestions. You should number these suggestions even if the reviewers did not number them; numbering them implies you have been extremely careful to cover all the reviewer's suggestions.)

If you disagree with what a reviewer wants, argue about it with the editor (who has selected the reviewer, by the way), not with the reviewer; and the editor could help with conflicts between reviewers. Appealing to the editor about rejection is sometimes successful in US journals but not often (Belcher 2009b), and couldn't doing so darken your name for future submissions and so raise the probability of your next article being sent to a Dr No reviewer?

Here is an example of a polite and conscientious reply to one reviewer with numbered points that *appears* to have incorporated everything the reviewer wanted; even when the reviewer was wrong, the would-be authors have tried to meet the reviewer half way and have not simply rejected their judgements (based on Bem (2002, p. 25)):

1. You suggested that we use multiple regression. But the authority Jones (2002, p. 45) says that multiple regression is as problematic as our ANOVA methodology. So we have retained our ANOVA analysis but added the results of a nonparametric analysis (which comes to the same conclusion). We could delete the ANOVA analysis and have only the nonparametric analysis, if you wish.
2. We have removed the old re-presentation of the four dimensions by merely putting them into a sentence on page 17 and not bullet pointing them, and removing their listing completely on page 30.
3. Thank you for noting that we have not made clear the differences between our cognitive approach and other's behavioural approach. So we have now included the word 'cognitive' in both the title and abstract, taken note of the debate about the two approaches in the introduction and stated explicitly there that the article will not undertake a comparative review of the two approaches. We hope this is satisfactory.

Thank you again for your help.

If the editor's decision is ***rejection***, do not give up—revise, recast and update, and submit to another journal! An author has to be resilient (Pannell 2002)! To handle the disappointment of rejection, some authors decide on a backup journal while they are deciding on a target journal, and so they know where the second submission will go as soon as they see the rejection message. How many rejections can an author expect? Authors can keep knocking on the door of about three to five journals in turn, before a journal finally accepts the article or the author finally gives up. Before it is submitted to that backup journal, the article ***must*** be *revised, recast and updated*, as noted. That is, all the suggestions of reviewers in the rejection journal have to be incorporated into the article for the next target journal; the article has to be recast for the backup journal to demonstrate that the journal has actually been targeted as the editor hopes it has been, in the four ways described above; and the reference list has to be updated so that recent articles in the new target journal and other journals are included. *All* previous reviewers' suggestions must be accepted because the same reviewer might review the article at the rejection journal *and* at the next journal, and so they will obviously reject it a second time if their previous suggestions have been ignored.

The major reason to keep submitting an (improved) article to a string of journals is that the peer review process is very, very flawed (Armstrong 1982, 1997; Pannell 2002; Saunders & Hirst 2000; Smith 2006). Some reviewers think they are perfect but reviewers are as imperfect as other humans. One study found the coefficient of determination between reviewers was a mere 0.2 (Fiske & Fogg 1990). Possibly, the flawed anonymous peer review process is used only because it is better than relying on the alternative of the editor's cronyism. The process is based on human behaviours in a context where innovation is required even though that innovation may upset the status quo to which the editor, members of the editorial board and the journal's readers are committed. In summary, one review of research about the peer review process concluded that the research showed the process was flawed, and that an article has to fit into the conversations of groups of like-minded academics and researchers:

> The literature on academic publishing produces *hardly any study that does not reveal failings* or condemns the process ... *Journals gather around like minded editors, reviewers and authors who meet at conferences*. Much research is pre-tested, knocked into shape or abandoned at such gatherings ... Within these communities, *researchers find collaborators who have complementary skills and who can share the burden of research*. (Saunders & Hirst 2000, p. 7; italics added)

Clearly, this empirical conclusion underlies the recommendations in this book chapter about forging long term relationships, targeting journals, going to conferences, and revising/recasting/updating before submitting to a backup journal after a rejection.

If an article has faced about three to five rejections after it has been revised, recast and updated after each submission, it should perhaps be dropped from an author's whiteboard portfolio. Perhaps reading Armstrong (1997) and Parnell (2002) would give the author new heart. But an author must write about incremental advances in future, that is, join a journal's conversation—do not upset conversants' beliefs, just politely extend them with important contributions.

CONCLUSION

In summary, article writing is a collaborative craft and is not an art or 'an abstract exercise aimed at inanimate objects' (Saunders & Hirst 2000, p. 1). Write in a conversation with known readers. Target the journal and aim to build a relationship with its editor, as well as with co-authors, colleagues who reciprocally review drafts, and friends in the track audience at conferences. Start with a team planning synopsis that includes appropriate target and backup journals, and have a structure/table of contents in that synopsis down to three numbered levels. Rough out the keywords, title, abstract and introduction. Set a deadline of two equivalent days to write the first draft. Then write the other three drafts, send off the article and revise it happily (or, if rejected, revise, recast and update, and try in the backup journal).

In conclusion, writing the first draft of an article may take two or so days, but planning and collecting data with colleagues beforehand, and then re-drafting it many times and revising it after the reviewers have looked at it, will all take many, many months. Thus following the processes above could bring the joy of acceptance into a conversation. And the long term relationships involved in the processes are a wonderful part of academic life. Indeed, the articles are tickets on intellectual journeys involving virtual and actual collaborations around the world. Bon voyages!

ACKNOWLEDGEMENTS

My training in the techniques of article writing began when I met two editors, David Carson and Audrey Gilmore, and this book chapter is closely based on articles co-authored with them. Other training sources were Abby Day's books and article and Robert Brown's article and book. Robert Brown kindly and very carefully reviewed a draft of this chapter, and Zoe Humborstad reviewed it, too. I thank all of them deeply.

PART B

EFFECTIVE RESEARCH:
HOW TO DO CASE, INTERVIEW AND ACTION RESEARCH

CHAPTER 3

HOW TO DO CASE RESEARCH:
A COMPREHENSIVE FRAMEWORK FOR MODERN RESEARCHERS

ABSTRACT

Case research is an emerging, non-traditional methodology and it is time to establish a comprehensive framework to guide modern academic researchers. The type of case research investigated here is realism case research executed by academic researchers. These case researchers should follow a seven-step systematic process that addresses: a how or why research problem about a social science situation and one to four research issues/propositions about the situation that emerge from the literature review; the appropriateness of the realism paradigm; a convergent interview first stage; a systematic investigation of four or so cases, selected with replication logic, using about 20 interviews (some of which are convergent interviews); thematic analysis of data from multiple sources of evidence; and analytic generalisation of the findings to extant theory about similar contexts. The framework presented strives to be effective by covering the essential steps, and to be also efficient by justifying where excessive work need not be done.

For acknowledgements and thanks, please refer to the end of this chapter.

INTRODUCTION

Case research is becoming more established. A Google Scholar search of the words 'case study research' in *Journal of Management Inquiry* for 2010 to 2011 uncovers 63 entries, while a similar search of the two years at the start of the century uncovers only 23. And *Academy of Management Review* (AMJ) confirms the growing impact of case research: 'papers that build theory from cases ... are among the most highly cited pieces in AMJ ... with impact disproportionate to their numbers' (Eisenhardt & Graebner 2007, p. 25). Similarly, *The Organisational Research Methods* journal notes that case research articles are 'frequently considered the "most interesting"' (Gibbert & Ruigrok 2010, p. 711). Furthermore, an introductory article about case research in *European Journal of Marketing* has amassed 451 citations, making that article into the thirteenth most-cited article of the thousands published in that journal (Perry 1998; Harzing 2007).

Despite this evidence about case research's growing importance, procedures for its use by academic case researchers are not established. Piekkari et al. (2007, p. 568) sum up this gap concerning academic research procedures: 'Although methodological texts on the case study have proliferated, they do not account for how this research strategy has actually been performed and practiced by management researchers'. Thus this book chapter aims to develop an integrated explanation of how case research about management can be done and reported. My contribution is the comprehensive framework developed for academic researchers in this one chapter, based on the realism paradigm and a modern stocktake of literature. My contributions include the establishment of how many interviews are required and the addition of a first research stage of a handful of initial 'convergent' interviews.

Essentially, I argue that case research solves and reports on a 'how' and/or 'why' research problem about a social science situation, and that it should be a seven-step, systematic investigation of that research problem. My framework will help the design and reporting of many articles and theses written by academics and their research students doing case research. Its foundations are the supervision of 17 doctoral theses and more than 7 journal articles.

This chapter has three parts. It begins with how the realism paradigm underlies much case research about enterprise management and marketing phenomena. Then a systematic approach to case research is developed. Finally, how case research fits into research programs is noted.

Here, the term 'case research' is viewed as a method or methodology and not more broadly as 'a transparadigmatic heuristic that enables the circumscription of the unit of analysis' (van Wynsberghe & Khan 2007, p. 90). In other words, case research is defined as a methodology that uses multiple sources of data to understand a phenomenon in its context to 'confront' theory with the real world (Piekkari 2007). The term 'case research' is used instead of the more usual terms of 'case study' or 'case study research' to distinguish this research from the descriptive 'stories' of case studies used in business school classes. Moreover, this case research focusses on disciplinary contexts like those of enterprise management and marketing, and that stance is justified in the first part of the chapter about the realism paradigm. However, there are many other situations where this type of case research could be done.

APPROPRIATENESS OF THE REALISM PARADIGM

A scientific paradigm underlies all research, whether it is acknowledged or not. So consider how the realism paradigm is the appropriate one for case research. (Readers who do not want to think about paradigms could skip directly to the next section about the steps of systematic case research.) A paradigm mirrors what is essential, legitimate and reasonable for a researcher. Scientific paradigms that guide research have been grouped into the four categories of positivism, critical theory, constructivism and realism (based on Guba & Lincoln 2005; explained fully in Perry, Riege & Brown 1999; Pawson & Tilley 1997; other paradigms are discussed in Palmer, Dick & Freiburger 2009; King & Horrocks 2010). These paradigms stretch between the two extremes of objective (positivism) and subjective (interpretivism); the realism paradigm of case research is midway between these two extremes, as shown in Figure 1 that illustrates many of the concepts to be raised here. In this section, each of these paradigms is compared for its appropriateness for research about interacting people in management situations, ending with the realism paradigm established as the most appropriate; this appropriateness drives the methodological steps developed later.

To begin, the **positivism** paradigm that dominates social science research assumes a tangible and apprehendable reality driven by laws (Guba and Lincoln 2005). Surveys and quantitative analysis of numbers are example methods within this paradigm for positivists use quantitative methods to precisely measure their decontextualized reality with zero measurement error for the dependent variable. The researcher views reality through a one-way mirror and so does not influence measurement of the phenomena—they are 'disintersted scientists' (Guba & Lincoln , 2005, p. 196). This paradigm is especially appropriate for engineers and others who work in the physical sciences with, for example, tangible bridges. However, in social science case research, the relationships and strategies that determine outcomes are not tangible or easily apprehendable constructs because the researcher is investigating many interacting humans, each of whom can learn from their experiences and change their behaviours (as can the researcher).

Figure 1 — A diagram of four scientific paradigms

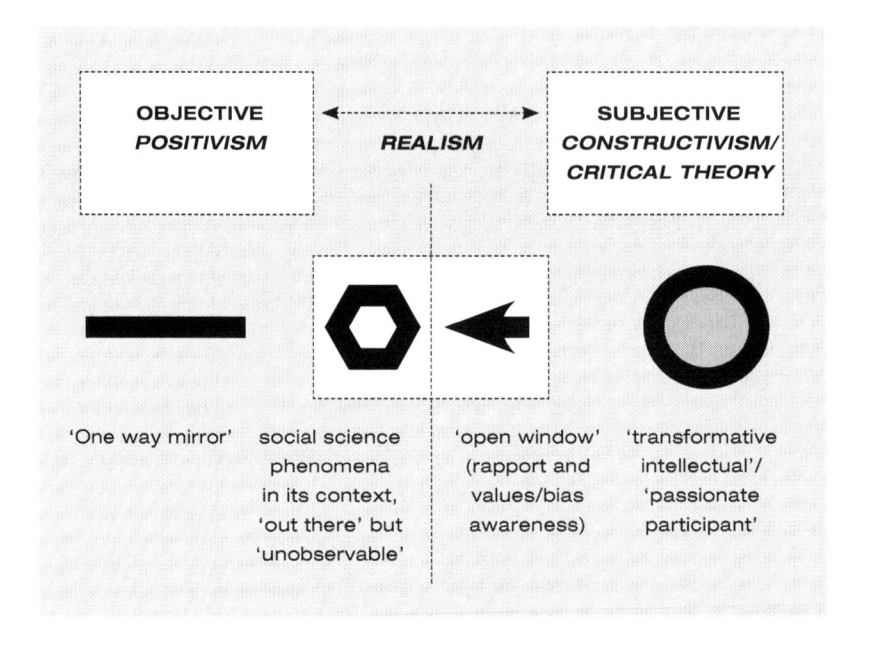

```
┌─────────────┐                    ┌──────────────────┐
│ OBJECTIVE   │ ◄─────────────►   │ SUBJECTIVE       │
│ POSITIVISM  │     REALISM       │ CONSTRUCTIVISM/  │
│             │                    │ CRITICAL THEORY  │
└─────────────┘                    └──────────────────┘
```

'One way mirror'   social science   'open window'   'transformative
                    phenomena   (rapport and   intellectual'/
                    in its context,   values/bias   'passionate
                    'out there' but   awareness)   participant'
                    'unobservable'

Note: The thin slice of *positivism* research reflects its more straightforward approach to reality than the approach in the three other types of research that search for more indepth complexities, and its closed boundary reflects its exclusion of the context around the physical phenomenon involved. The heavy boundary around the subjective realities of *constructivism and critical theory* reflects the relativism of such research—the findings cannot apply in other situations. *Realism* is in the middle between the two extremes and has a thin boundary to indicate that it incorporates the context of social science phenomena, that is, it is context-dependent. Realism has a 'light' on the left and an 'arrow' pointing towards it; the light reflects realism's concern about an 'objective' world that was created by humans but exists independently of them, and the arrow reflects how an investigation of its situations usually requires some 'subjective' perceptions from people.

Nevertheless, most business school research adopts this positivism paradigm although it is hardly ever read by managers (Matchett 2010). Managers use more context-inclusive thinking than positivism researchers do (Flyvberg 2006) and so positivism research may be especially inappropriate for reaching the management development aims of professional doctorates in some business-related fields (Perry 2011).

That the irrelevance of positivism research has not affected its traditional role in business school research might be explained in neuroscience terms. Positivism can be linked with the left hemisphere of the brain through its emphasis on abstraction and breaking wholes into parts. This left hemisphere is logical and consistent but decontextualized and narrow—'The left hemisphere [is] an ambitious bureaucrat with their own interests at heart ... the left hemisphere has a narrow, decontextualised and theoretically based model of the world which is self-consistent and is therefore quite powerful' (McGilchrist 2010, p. 3).

Two alternative paradigms to positivism are the opposite, subjective end of an objective/subjective continuum: the interpretive paradigms of constructivism and critical theory. **Constructivism** is based on multiple constructed realities, that is, subjective realities of many individuals; ethnography and participant observation are example methodologies within this paradigm. A constructivism researcher maps the perceived realities of an individual—there is no reality as important as that created by the individual's own awareness. Thus constructivism researchers are 'passionate participants' in the research project (Guba & Lincoln 2005, p. 196). But one cannot judge between each subjective perception of respondents and so a researcher must remain a relativist, that is, a finding from one respondent may not apply to any other person. In neuroscience terms, this paradigm 'often comes to mean there is no truth at all. There is nothing out there beyond the sort of paintings on the wall of the inside of our mind ... the world appears to be a heap of fragments' (McGilchrist 2009, p. 11). However, *one* individual's meanings attributed to case research phenomena do not independently decide the strategic outcomes of an enterprise in the external world, for an enterprise's several internal and external stakeholders decide these outcomes (Gummesson 2000).

Similarly, the other interpretive paradigm of **critical theory** downplays the existence of a window to an outside reality or truth; instead, perception by a group is the reality; action research and ethnography are example methodologies within this paradigm. Within critical theory, reality and knowledge are altered over time by structural/historical insights and the researcher may change the mental world in which respondents live, that is, the researcher becomes a 'transformative intellectual' (Guba & Lincoln 2005, p. 196). Much management case research aims to map perceptions that can be generalised out to other similar situations, and it does not intend to shape or alter a perceived reality—the researcher does not aim to be a transformative intellectual within one group. (Another interpretive paradigm of 'participatory' is added to critical theory and constructivism in the third edition of Lincoln and Guba (2005) but it is close to the two interpretive paradigms above and so including it here would not help in understanding realism's appropriateness for case research.) In brief, the three paradigms above are inappropriate for much management research.

So consider the fourth paradigm of **realism** that is appropriate for case research. The realism position is that explanatory knowledge is sought (Easton 1998) of a real social science world that is difficult to measure and is somewhat independent of researchers; moreover, there are many perceptions of the world by people and these perceptions need to be triangulated to develop an approximate picture of the reality. That is, reality is not finally known like it is supposed to be in positivism; realism researchers recognise that they merely aim at further development of prior theory and so move our understanding *closer* to the truth, although precise knowledge of that reality will always remain uncertain (Perry et al. 1999). One reason for that imprecision is that the context of the situation can affect the findings.

Essentially, the realism researcher observes people through an 'open window'—it is not a one-way mirror that hides the researcher from the people, but nor does it allow people to be as close to the researcher as they are when 'co-researchers' of interpretive research. That is, in the case research process, the researcher has to reduce bias in the people and in themselves, as much as possible. This world consists of abstract things that are born of people's minds but exist independently of any one person—'the third world is largely autonomous, though created by us' (Popper 1985, p. 61). For example, there is a world 'out there' in which relationships exist between stakeholders and these external influences determine the outcomes of enterprise strategies more than the subjective preferences of managers or any one other person do—'The real decisions are made in the world outside—among consumers, middlemen, competitors, politicians, legislators and trade organisations' (Gummesson 2000, p.105). In other words, the realism paradigm is an appropriate worldview with which to investigate many phenomena in the fields of enterprise management and marketing, and many other phenomena that are midway between the objectivism of positivism and the subjectivism of contructivism and critical theory.

Note that there are at least two types of case research that reflect the differences between two of these paradigms. The differences between realism and constructivism are captured in Stake's (2005) distinction between intrinsic and instrumental case research. Ragin (1997; Pikkeir et al. 2007) describes the two types as case-oriented and variable-oriented. In *intrinsic*/case-oriented case research, the case itself is the focus. Thus often only a single case is researched to gather deep information about the case. In contrast, in instrumental/realism case research, the case is being used to understand something else than the cases *per se*. In this type of case research, often more than one case is investigated to understand processes that occur in several case situations. (Note that the theories about these processes in realism case research occur within the particular types of the cases and their contexts, and are not thought to be theories about processes that operate 'regardless of context' (as suggested in Pikkeir et al. 2007, p. 570)—the theories are in the middle between the two extremes of one case's context and no context at all (Eisenhardt & Graebner 2007, p. 25). In other words, a participant's perceptions are being studied for their own sake in intrinsic/constructivism research and so the participant's perceptions drive data collection and analysis; but in instrumental/realism research, these perceptions are being studied because they provide glimpses of some thing *beyond* those perceptions—the external reality that enterprise management and marketing researchers, for example, want to understand (Gummeson 2000).

In brief, realism case research is especially appropriate for situations like many of those in enterprise management and marketing research, and provides a framework of ontology and epistemology to investigate their complex social world.

SYSTEMATIC CASE RESEARCH

Steps 1 and 2: The research problem and its research issues
The discussion of realism above provides an understanding of the seven steps in systematic case research about, for example, an enterprise management or marketing phenomenon: (1) the research problem and its research issues; (2) the realism paradigm and justification of the case research method; (3) identifying a case and their number; (4) multiple sources of evidence, including interviews, collected over two stages; (5) quality; (6) data analysis; and (7) analytic generalisation. Each step needs to be addressed during the research project. They need not be described in full detail in an article, so long as their presence is acknowledged by

some mention of them all (with cited supporting references), but each step should be discussed in detail in a thesis.

First, in realism research, the overriding research problem must be about a relatively complex, difficult-to-measure social science phenomenon involving people. One way of ensuring an overall research problem is an appropriate one is to frame it as a 'how' or 'why' problem that cannot be answered with a simple yes or no; and it must be about a real world, context-dependent situation and not be about an abstraction (Yin 2009). Case research is 'midrange' between the details of just one situation and the genralisation of concepts that are thought to apply to all situations (Ozcan & Eisenhardt 2009, p. 253). For example, case research could be about a type of event or project, or be about a relationship between marketing managers in a supply chain. One way of testing this context-dependency is to check if these questions about the problem can be answered: who is involved, what do they do, where do they do it, and when do they do it (Yin 2009)? The answers could be incorporated into the wording of the research problem or explicitly noted in a delimitations section. Two examples of appropriate research problem are: 'How and why do inter-organisational relationships of public sector events agencies impact upon events tourism strategy making within Australian states and territories?' (Stokes 2003, p. ii); and 'How do doctors manage hospitals competently?' with more details about that problem incorporated into a delimitations section (Loh 2012, p. ii).

The prior theory about that research problem situation must be explored in a literature review to show the gaps could be illuminated by the case research. Those gaps are described in only 2 to 4 'research issues' or 'propositions'. They are called research issues or propositions rather than 'hypotheses' to indicate they are more inductive than the deductive hypotheses of positivism research. For example, the literature review in one article had a research problem involving internationalisation and innovation, and had covered theories about these in the literature before identifying three research issues that were worth investigating:

> In summary the three different streams of literature on internationalization, innovation and networks show that internationalization and innovation are linked ... however, we identified various gaps. Consequently, we aim to identify the following:
> - the type of internationalization and whether it is radical or incremental;
> - the type of innovation and whether it is radical or incremental; and

- the type of network relationships and how they are used by these firms to innovate and to internationalize. (Chetty & Stangl 2010, p. 1729)

This emphasis on background, prior theory shows that case research can be a *theory testing* or theory confirming method (justified above), and not a mere lead-in to more 'serious', quantitative theory testing (Yin 2009). Moreover, this emphasis makes clear the case research does not operate in intrinsic, constructivism or critical theory paradigms (that is, intrinsic case research (Stake 2005)). Essentially, in theory testing case research, the researcher tests whether the patterns in the case data match those in the theory. Note that case research and quantitative methods test different type of theories about different types of phenomena (captured in their types of research problem described above), and that distinction is the only difference between their stand alone, theory-testing capability. Each method could be a lead-in to the other.

After the literature review ends in this research issues way, the methodology section begins to outline the six other case research steps that were followed in the research project. The section begins with the appropriateness of the realism paradigm and should be described along the lines of the realism section above. Then the particular type of case research methodology should be acknowledged and justified, such as interview-based multiple case research (Pierreki et al. 2007). An often used way of doing this justification is to refer to the why or how form of the research question, that control over behavioural events was not possible, and that events were contemporaneous (Yin 2009, p. 8). This justification of the case research methodology is needed because the qualitative data produced in the case research project may make some readers confused about the method used to collect that data. Indeed, it is best to not use the term 'qualitative research' because so many different approaches are covered by that term (Eisenhardt & Graebner 2009).

Step 3: Identifying a case and their number

The third systematic step is identifying what constitutes 'a case' or the unit of analysis, and deciding on the number of cases. A **case** in realism case research should be a real social science phenomenon and not an abstraction, for example, a case could be a decision by managers or a project involving people (Yin 2009). One or more principles of case selection can be used, for example, maximum variation (the most commonly used principle), intensity, homogeneous and typical (Patton 2002, pp. 243-244). But the core consideration is that the case should be at a level of detail that is appropriate for the research problem, that is, what you want to make analytic generalisations about. For an example of how a case researcher decided on what constituted a case, consider a researcher who was investigating how doctors become hospital managers (Loh 2011). Was his case 'a hospital' or 'a doctor'? After some initial interviews (described in step 4 below) and reading, and after thinking about the considerations in the paragraph above, the researcher eventually decided that a case was 'role of a doctor/manager in the context of a particular type of hospital'. Next, would those roles be present in public or private hospitals, or both? Furthermore, would the contexts of the doctor/manager roles be the same in all hospitals in the state where the cases were situated, or in hospitals in the whole country, or in hospitals in other countries as well? In other words, what were the *delimitations* of the case research? After some thought and reading, it was decided that the roles were in the same context throughout the state and the country, but that different cultures, health systems and doctor training could affect generalisation beyond them to hospitals in other countries. This thinking process is an example of how the research problem and the boundaries of the cases nearly always evolve in the early stages of a case research project (Dubois & Araujo 2004). In brief, 'redirecting ... case [research] may involve incorporation of additional theory and redefinitions of the unit of analysis, including its spatial and temporal boundaries' (Piekkari et al. 2007, p. 573).

After the nature of a case is determined, the **number of cases** can be decided. The number is usually about 4 or so cases: more than this number makes data analysis and reporting too word-consuming; and less than this number limits the analytic generalisation that can be done because their too-few contexts make the generalisation too shallow or narrow. For example, if the number of cases is more than 10, say, the depth of information about each case in the report's dense tables is actually so 'shallow' that the usual richness of case research is lost, and so the research should be called something like a 'limited-depth cross-sectional field study' (Lillis & Mundy 2005; cited in Piekkari et al. 2007). And if there are fewer than about 4 cases or so in extrinsic/realism case research, then the construct validity provided by triangulation across several cases is diminished.

Indeed, to investigate just one case needs to be justified on at least one, and hopefully more, of these five criteria in Yin (2009, pp. 47-50): the case must be

1. a critical one for testing all the conditions of a theory (for example, the Cuban crisis faced by President Kennedy)
2. an extreme or unique case (that is, a rare case)
3. a representative or typical case (for generalising about experiences of an average situation)

4. a revelatory case (that was previously inaccessible to researchers), and/or
5. a longitudinal case (the same case at different periods; in effect, the periods become many 'sub-cases' of the single case).

By the way, an *'embedded'* case is a sub-case of a case, and embedded cases must be analysed and their overall picture established before other pictures can be compared with that picture (Yin 2009). For example, the departments of a firm could be embedded cases, that is, sub-cases of the case of a firm that have to be assessed before the firms can be compared with other firms. However, using the term 'case' for both levels of case can be confusing for both a reader and a writer, and so the term 'sub-case' could be preferred.

A major influence on deciding the number of cases in multiple-case research is *replication logic*, that is, each case is carefully selected so that it would produce similar results as another case (literal replication) or different results in another case (theoretical replication), for *a priori* reasons (Carson et al. 2001; Yin 2009). This logic captures the context of the cases and allows more informed analytic generalisation, that is, it improves the quality of the case research project.

For example, in the doctor/manager case research described above, the replication logic identified five cases/types of hospital that should have been investigated. That logic used three dimensions of context to ensure interviewees were chosen for each type of hospital; whether the hospital was public or private; whether it was a general or specialist hospital; and its location in the city, suburbs or out in a region. The researcher explained his replication logic in detail:

> ... cases were selected according to the type of hospital employing the doctor in a senior hospital management role. The five cases are based on the role of a doctor in a senior management role in five different hospital locations and types: metropolitan public, suburban public, rural/regional public, private and specialist hospital. These organisations are similar in that they are all hospitals in [my state], with similar organisational structures and operational functions, but are also different because of their sizes, location and way they are funded. Therefore, there are three replication dimensions ... Dimension 1 is based on the funding of the hospital, that is, whether the hospital is public or private. Dimension 2 is the type of hospital, whether it is general or specialist. Dimension 3 is the location of the hospital, whether it is metropolitan, suburban, or rural/regional.

In this way, we can expect theoretical replication when predicted differences are observed and literal replication when there is confirmation of similarities. The 3 dimensions are summarised in Table [I]. Other types of cases were not investigated because there are no hospitals with other combinations of dimensions. For example, not all hospitals have a chief medical officer, or a doctor in the chief executive officer position.

Table I — Three dimensions of theoretical and literal replication

DIMENSION 1: FUNDING		PUBLIC		PRIVATE	
DIMENSION 2: TYPE		General	Specialist	General	Specialist
DIMENSION 3: LOCATION	Metropolitan	A	D	E	X
	Suburban	B	X	E	E
	Rural/regional	C	X	X	X

Note: X = no interviewees due to absence of hospitals … with those dimensions or absence of doctors in senior hospital management roles in some types of hospitals.

Step 4: Multiple sources of evidence, including interviews collected over two stages
The fourth systematic case research step is the sources of evidence. *Multiple* sources of evidence are used in case research because it explores the indepth complexities of situations, and no one source overwhelms the benefits of others. The most usual source of evidence is semi-structured interviews but other sources must be included and they could be documents scavenged at interview sites and from the Internet, direct observation, and even 'participant-observation, and physical artefacts. [Moreover] case studies can include, and even be limited to, quantitative evidence' (Yin 2009, p. 19). (But note that the quantitative results of a Internet-based survey (for example, a survey that used Survey Monkey) would provide statistical generalisation that would be delimited to the case's population itself, and

the analytic generalisation provided by the many non-survey sources of case research would be needed to extend this statistical generalisation about the one case, as step 7 explains.) Researchers should try to use at least two or three of these sources of data.

Because **interviews** are usually the main source of case research evidence, a key question is: 'How many interviews are enough?' To begin, interviewees are chosen for their relevance rather than for their representativeness like respondents in a random survey sample are—the interviewees are 'purposefully' chosen because they are rich in information about the case (Patton 2002, p. 46), and the differences between the number of interviewees for each case is irrelevant (thus using quantitative words like 'sample' when referring to selection of interviewees in qualitative research can be confusing). However, the number of interviewees in each case is usually around about the same. The answer to how many of these interviewees in total are required revolves around the concept of 'saturation' when no new information or patterns in the data emerge from the interviews (Guest, Bunce & Johnson 2006). This saturation depends on the type of research problem, the cases themselves, the skill of the interviewer, the depth of data analysis, and so on. Patton (2002, p. 245) summarises this difficulty of deciding how many interviews are needed: 'The validity, meaningfulness and insights generated from qualitative inquiry have more to do with the information-richness of the cases selected and the observational/analytical capabilities of the researcher than with sample size.'

Thus estimates of the *required total number of interviews* vary. For example, the minimum can be about 6 (Guest, Bunce & Johnson 2008; Morse 2000), 10 (de Ruyter & Scholl 1998) or 15 (Betraux 1981 in Guest et al. 2008). The maximum can be about 50 (de Ruyter & Scholl 1998; Mason 2010). A number less than 10 is usually appropriate if the emphasis is on within-case analysis, and more is needed if the emphasis is on the cross-case analysis usually involved with 4 or so cases (Clark & Gibbs 2008). Overall, the usually accepted number of interviews in a research project is around 15 to 25 (Charmaz 2006; Green & Thorogood 2004; Gaskell 2000; Crawford & Di Benetto 2008). For example, Gaskell (2000, p. 44) says that between 15 and 25 interviews is appropriate:

> ...there is an upper limit to the number of interviews that it is necessary to conduct and possible to analyse. For the single researcher this is somewhere between 15 and 25 individual interviews ... Of course the research may be phased: a first set of interviews, followed by analysis, and then a second set.

This number of between 15 and 25 interviews relies on the skill of the interviewer, on their development of appropriate questions, and on the thoroughness of their data analysis. One handy way of ensuring these are done at a high standard is to use **convergent interviewing** in a first stage of a case research project (Dick 1998; described in detail in this book's Chapter 4 about interviewing and in Rao & Perry 2003, 2007). These initial convergent interviews can be held with *experts* like academics or consultants, to help refine the topics that will be raised in all the later, second stage case interviews with *practitioners*. The convergent interviews can be done while the literature review is being written and ideas from the literature can be incorporated into their questions. Any points of convergence or divergence among interviewees are examined *after each* convergent interview to develop the questions and probes for the next interview. These evolving convergent questions focus on what are the main topics that could affect each research issue in turn. The final convergent interview has occurred when interview data analysis of that interview shows there is a consistent pattern of agreements and disagreements in the last two interviews (Carson et al. 2001; Rao & Perry 2003, 2007). This saturation or 'stability' is usually reached after only five or so convergent interviews; it can be seen in a matrix that has interviewees on one axis and the three to five main topics for each research issue progressively uncovered in the interviews on the other axis, and the last two columns for the last two interviewees will have entries in each cell. (That matrix needs to be merely mentioned in an article but it could be described and explained in detail in a thesis.)

This first convergent interviewing stage with experts ensures the interviewer becomes more skilled, and ensures the appropriateness of the research issues and interview questions in the later case interviews with practitioners (and helps the development of codes for data analysis, as is discussed later). Convergent interviews also help in deciding on the cases to research in the second stage. As well, as described in the doctor/manager research mentioned above, this first convergent interviewing stage in the gradual evolution of case research is a way of ensuring the quality of data collection and analysis. That is, the convergent interviewing stage helps ensure that the later case interviewing stage with practitioners does not stumble upon the problem of uncovering completely new concepts that would mean answers to all the questions in all the previous case interviews could not be compared (and so the interviews done before the stumble would have to be ignored). This 'stumbles' situation in case research can be called the 'serendipity and emerging problem' (Gibbert & Ruigrok 2010, p. 730). And Patton (2002, p. 44) relates this problem to the 'emergent design flexibility' of all qualitative research; he gave an example of how he discovered part way through a project that his group had split into two groups and he suddenly had to decide—mid-stream, so to speak—which group to follow. A first convergent interviewing stage of case research helps to ensure this problem does not happen in your case research project.

In brief, case research should have a first stage of about 5 convergent interviews with experts, and can have about 15 or so second stage case interviews with practitioners (that is, about 3 or 4 triangulating interviews in each of about 4 or 5 cases), to make a total of about 20 interviews. So the conclusion to a case research report about the number of interviews could cite some of the references above and summarise with a sentence like this one:

> The 19 interviews in this research project is an appropriate number because of the convergence that was carefully sought in the 5 convergent interviews of stage 1, and the thoroughness of the data analysis of the 14 second stage case interviews in the Findings section below.

Of course, case researchers should use common interviewing techniques in both stages such as having an interviewer's guide that covers steps like breaking the ice, ethics clearances, broad questions leading to probe questions, active listening and the conclusion (Carson et al. 2001; King & Horrocks 2010; Patton 2002). Incidentally, listening to a tape recording of an interview allows the interviewer to check their notes (for careful note-taking is required even when a tape recorder is used) (Patton 2002, pp. 380-384). Interviewing techniques like these apply to all qualitative methods of research and are covered in detail in this book's Chapter 4.

But do these interview techniques in case research include computer-assisted analysis of expensive and time-consuming transcripts of the tapes of the case research interviews? Several authorities argue such computer assistance is not essential. For example, Yin (2009, p. 129; italics added) says, '... even under the best of circumstances, *nearly all scholars* express *strong caveats* about any use of the computer-assisted tools'. And Patton (2002, p. 446; italics added) concurs: 'So although software analysis has become common and many swear by it ... it is *not a requisite* for qualitative inquiry'. The reasons for not insisting on computer-assisted analysis center on the fact that meanings can be lost because in computer-assisted analysis, the case interview data could be treated as decontextualized blocks of information rather than as inter-connected wholes. Computer-assisted analysis may be efficient with data from more interviews than are advocated here and it is probably essential in constructivism or critical theory paradigm research; but it is not essential in realism paradigm research like the case research here because realism does not focus on mental constructions per se, but on the external world that the interviewees perceive (Sobh & Perry 2006).

Step 5: Quality of the research
The fifth step in systematic case research should be assessing the quality or rigor of the research. Researchers could do that step by covering King and Horrock's (2010, pp. 1616-165) or Healy and Perry's (2000) detailed establishment of quality criteria for realism research that are more appropriate for case research than those of positivism (Yin 2009) and interpretivism (Lincoln & Guba 1985) paradigm research.

The first two of Healy and Perry's realism criteria concern ontological appropriateness and contingent validity. The third criterion concerns epistemology: handling possible bias in the multiple perceptions of participants and of researchers through triangulation. The researcher has to become aware of their sources' and their own values, and allow for how those values may be slanting each person's perceptions of the outside reality that is being researched; building rapport during interviews assists here, as do the second and third phases of the data analysis step to be described next. The final three criteria concern methodology: methodological trustworthiness, analytic generalization and construct validity. Another widely-used alternative set of quasi-positivism quality criteria in Yin (2009, pp. 40-45): construct validity, internal validity, external validity and reliability.

Showing an awareness of at least some of all these quality criteria is a bare minimum requirement of case research reports. Moreover, the report should focus on the 'concrete actions' taken to ensure quality, and should prioritize various concepts of internal validity and reliability over external validity (Gibbert & Rugriok 2010, p. 725) (because external validity is usually concerned with positivism's statistical generalization and not with the analytic generalization of realism's case research covered in step 7 below). Of course, all researchers should also mention how they addressed ethical issues.

Step 6: Data analysis
The sixth step in systematic case research is data analysis. Tables are necessary here to capture details for the text of a thesis (an article covers only core ideas). There are five phases involved in usual case research data analysis: familiarization, coding, developing themes in the coded data, establishing major themes, and reporting. The first phase involves becoming familiar

with the mounds of information gathered from the interviews and other sources (Patton 2002). The researcher reads through field notes and any interview transcripts to develop an initial understanding of the content of the interviews. This first reading of the data is carried out without making any notes about themes or commonalities that may have emerged from the data. (In effect, this phase is a pre-'open coding' pass in Neuman's terminology (2007, p. 408), or a 'get a sense of the whole' first pass in Patton's terminology (2002, p. 440).)

During this first phase, the researcher can write the *within-case* analysis for each case, that is, a description of each case in tables and brief text to allow the reader to understand the background of later quotations (sometimes some cases need to be somewhat disguised to protect confidentiality). This within-case analysis is sometimes called 'the research setting' (for example, in Ozcan & Eisenhardt 2009).

Next, having familiarized themselves with the data and having made initial notes, the researcher sets about the second phase of placing **codes** or 'conceptual categories' on the words, sentences or paragraphs in the data (Neuman 2007, p. 330); these codes can overlap. The first codes used will have been identified from previous theory, that is, from the research issues, from the convergent interview findings and from the interview questions (Gibbs & Taylor 2010). For example, if there are three research issues at the end of the literature review and about four topics were identified under each research issue in the earlier convergent interview stage, there may be 12 codes. But other codes will then emerge from the data as the researcher's understanding of the data increases, that is, extra codes from the data emerge as the researcher puts aside conceptions and previous knowledge of the topic. During this process, coding is changing its emphasis from description to interpretation or analysis (*why* things were happening) (King & Horrocks 2010). About 50 codes are usually more than enough (Gibbs & Taylor 2010). By the way, this procedure is different from grounded theory where all the codes come only from the data, and so the term 'grounded theory' should not be used in case research reports (Oznac & Eisenhardt 2009).

Now comes the third phase where higher-level patterns (categories and sub-categories) in the coded data are developed, that is, overarching **themes** in the coded data. In other words, broad themes rise above earlier, narrower, more specific coded data (Clarke & Gibbs 2008). (This phase is equivalent to the 'selective coding' pass of Neuman (2007, p. 332) and is part of 'thematic analysis' in King & Horrocks (2010, pp. 152-158).) For example, the theme of 'information quality' could arise from codes about 'accuracy', 'currency', 'specificity', 'sufficiency' and 'variety'. Continuous cycles of testing codes and their themes against the data are a characteristic of case research and show it is fallacious to criticize case research as being too 'subjective' (Flyvberg 2006 , p. 235)—case research demands 'close adherence to the data... keeping researchers *"honest"* (Eisenhardt & Graebner 2007, p. 27; italics added). As well as this cycling of interpretation against data, two other ways to stop data analysis degenerating into reinforcement of a researcher's own prejudices are to use prior theory as in step 1 above, and to explicitly test rival or alternative explanations of results during the analysis (these explanations are often triggered by disagreements between interviewees that an initial data analysis uncovers). Throughout the research project, a researcher should be aware of their own values and biases (Easterby-Smith et al. 2008).

After these themes are uncovered, the fourth phase of data analysis can establish a final set of even higher-order **major themes** (or meta-themes) that arise from the more numerous themes of the third phase; these major themes are present in all or most cases (Gibbs & Taylor 2010) and provide direct answers to the research issues. The optimal number of these major themes would vary with the report's word length, the data, and the nature of the research problem and its research issues. But it is generally about 2 to 5 themes for an article (King & Horrocks 2010, p. 158; Rocco & Pltahotnik 2011) or about 10 to 15 themes for a doctoral thesis. An article writer may not have to summarise these themes into one overall conceptual framework with the usual circles and arrows, for space reasons, but a thesis writer should do so.

After these major themes have been developed, the final phase is **reporting** them in an article or thesis. That is, the Findings section is structured around the themes that have been uncovered (and/or the research issues). Discussions of themes (or the 'wood') are presented first, and then more detailed support of them (or the 'trees') is presented, such as quotations, to confirm the trustworthiness of the themes being discussed. These details include some notes about the testing of rival or alternative explanations of the findings. Of course, these details do not include frequencies or proportions in the data, because this is qualitative research and not survey research.

Qualitative data is distinctive because it is 'rich' and many readers of reports of qualitative research expect many details of its 'rich empirical evidence', such as quotations, in a research report (Eisenhardt & Graebner 2007, p. 29). But case research data analysis has to develop theories as well as describe a rich picture, and so readers more interested in theory than in the richness in the quotations can skim some of the quotations; indeed, they might concentrate on:

- the research issues and themes that provide the structure for the cross-case analysis
- the matrices that summarise the findings
- the summary in the first sentence of most paragraphs
- the paraphrase at the beginning of most quotations
- the short conclusion summary at the end of each sub-section
- the section after the final research issue that summarises all of the sections with the quotations.

Confirming this necessary emphasis on theory development over evidence, *The Handbook of Scholarly Writing and Publishing* (Rocco & Plathotnik 2011, p. 173; italics added) notes: 'The meaning that readers should take from the data should be introduced *prior to the data*. After the data have been presented, a *transition* is needed to the next idea or chunk of data'.

All this reporting of the data analysis focusses on *cross-case* and on *cross-cluster* analysis (if an article's word limits allow the latter) to derive a deeper understanding of the cases' similarities and differences; doing this analysis of rival patterns across cases raises insights that help address the research issues. The cross-case analysis compares all the cases. In turn, any cross-cluster analysis compares clusters of interviewees or cases, with the clustering based on the dimensions used for replication logic or on groups of cases or interviewees that provided different patterns of responses; for example, clusters could be interviewees from big and from small enterprises. These cross-case and cross-cluster analyses are based on summary tables that display the data in the form of matrices. While starting to condense the data set to these manageable and detailed structures, the researcher can return to the data sources to extract more information or rearrange the layout.

Step 7: Analytic generalisation
The seventh and final step in systematic case research is the *analytic* generalisation that occurs in the Discussion section after the Findings section—'The final step in analysis [is] to place these findings within a wider perspective' (Kasper, Lehrer, Muhlbacher & Muller 2010, p. 375). Analytic generalisation is a form of external validation. At least one examiner of a case research thesis or one reviewer of a case research article will probably think that external validity is a serious limitation of case research, so a case researcher may as well address the issue before the examiner or reviewer does. The case researcher could address it by distinguishing

between analytic generalisation and statistical generalisation (Yin 2009, pp. 15, 38-40, 43-44). Case research does not *statistically* generalise to a sampled population; in contrast to that minor form of generalisation, case research produces a theory that can be *analytically* generalised (adds) to other theories about somewhat similar contexts (Yin 2009). The external validity of case research is first addressed in its use of prior theory and replication logic for designing multiple cases to address research issue arising from the literature, and these are the foundations of the analytic generalisation in case research. Because statistical generalisation in a survey or experiment generalises only to the sampled population, it takes several such quantitative studies to extend that generalisation to other populations. Providing analytic generalisation in one multiple-case research project is somewhat equivalent to doing all those repeat studies *at once*. That is, the analytic generalisation in the Discussion section of a case research report has a more important role than it does in other research reports where it simply folds the findings into the extant literature. In brief, discussion of theories about similar contexts is an important part of the Discussion section of a case research report.

The Discussion section has many citations and that previous literature is not denigrated in any way—this research fits around previous researchers and extends them by using words like 'extends', 'adds to', 'augments', 'explains', contributes' and so on. An example of how this analytic generalisation is done in a case research report is in Gross & Pullman (2012).

After that analytic generalisation, the Discussion section covers the usual issues of implications for scholars, managers and policy makers, and limitations and further research.

IMPLICATIONS FOR RESEARCH PROGRAMS

An implication of the above discussion is that case research can be as straightforward and rigorous as quantitative research claims to be. Thus the realism paradigm and the seven steps in this chapter could be taught in all graduate research training programs; and kept in mind when theses and articles are written, and when they are evaluated by thesis examiners and article reviewers.

As noted in the section about the realism paradigm, the type of case research discussed here is often appropriate in fields like those of enterprise management and marketing, and so other types of case research may be more appropriate for other fields like psychology, organisational behaviour and education that frequently operate within the constructivism and critical theory paradigms. However, there may be many research projects in these other fields where the realism paradigm is appropriate.

In particular, case research has strong implications for a professional doctorate dissertation, especially for a manager doing the Doctor of Business Administration (DBA) professional doctorate (Perry 2011). Managers are not aiming at establishing an academic career measured by journal articles, but at furthering their professional management career. They must select a research problem and methodology that fits that aim. That is, the rationale for a DBA should be that the degree develops the manager's **practice**. *The Australian Qualifications Framework* explicitly notes this distinction: 'The research Doctoral Degree (typically referred to as a PhD) makes a significant and original contribution to knowledge; the professional Doctoral Degree (typically titled Doctor of (field of study)) makes a significant and original contribution to knowledge in the context of professional practice.' (*Australian Qualifications Framework* 2011, p. 52)

Thus, I argue that DBA research cannot simply apply any old, standard PhD methodology—it should apply only an inductive, theory-building methodology like case research (Yin 2008; Perry 1998b). As noted above, case research has a 'how' and/or 'why' research problem rather than a 'what' research problem (Yin 2008), and thus includes the underlying mechanisms of dynamic situations. In particular, the research problem should be about what managers *do* and include some reference to the context, like 'How can funeral homes market their services in Australia?' (Morelli 2010) and 'How can a healthcare supply chain be managed, with particular reference to an armed forces healthcare supply chain in Malaysia?' (Basari 2009).

That is, case research is more in-depth and context-aware than survey research. For example, a survey would provide evidence about how many people prefer one political party over others, but case research would provide the deeper evidence that the party's managers need for them to work out *how* to change those preferences. And DBA case research involves the context-dependent knowledge that is required for the development of rule-based beginners into the 'virtuoso' experts that management development aims at (Flyvberg 2008, p. 221). Even if a part of the evidence collected in DBA research is constructivist (for example, ethnography) or critical theory (for example, action research), the degree's major focus should be on the *management* of such evidence and so should be primarily positioned within the realism paradigm (Zuber-Skerritt & Perry 2009). For example, one DBA candidate's 'cases' were some of his training courses within companies, and he used data from participant observation, interviews and documents as his sources of information for a case research thesis. Other candidates could use the strategic planning process with their firm as their case, or several marketing plans they have done as a consultant as their cases.

In contrast to the case research above, most published research from business schools is theory-based and theory-testing, and these articles in academic journals (for which a PhD trains candidates to write) are actually irrelevant for most business people (Skapinker 2008); presumably, most PhD research is the same. Indeed, this mainstream research from most business schools is hardly ever read by managers, as noted by a global accrediting agency for business schools (and this book's Chapter 3):

> ...AACSB International, the most widely recognised global accrediting agency for business schools, announced it would consider changing the way it evaluates research. The news followed rather damning criticism in 2002 ... which questioned whether business education in its current guise was sustainable... Most of the research is highly quantitative, hypothesis-driven and esoteric. As a result, it is almost universally unread by real-world managers. (The Economist 2007)

CONCLUSION

In summary, case research builds theories, rather than merely test theories like research within the positivism paradigm does. Moreover, it is positioned within the realism paradigm rather than alternative inductive paradigms of constructivism and critical theory. As noted above, the world view of realism consists of abstract things that are born of people's minds but exist independently of any one person (Perry, Riege & Brown 1999; Perry 2004) and is about an external reality that exists within a dynamic framework of interacting people. Realism is especially appropriate for most management research because many of its phenomena are determined in the external reality of a marketplace, and not by the subjective constructions of constructivism and critical theory. To describe this case research, this chapter has established seven steps that cover: a how or why research problem about a social science situation, and one to four research issues/propositions about the situation that emerge from the literature review; the appropriateness of the realism paradigm; a convergent interview first stage; a systematic investigation of 4 or so cases selected with replication logic, with its 20 interviews (some of which are convergent interviews);

thematic analysis of data from multiple sources of evidence; and analytic generalisation of the findings to extant theory about similar contexts.

In conclusion, case research is appropriate for in-depth investigations of social science phenomena in fields like enterprise management and marketing, and others. This case research is based on theory, follows systematic and straightforward procedures, and extends extant theory through its analytic generalisation. And it can be conducted and reported in ways that are both effective and efficient.

ACKNOWLEDGEMENTS

I thank Drs Robyn Stokes and Erwin Loh for comments on an early draft of this chapter, and my many doctoral and other postgraduate research students for helping me to develop these ideas. I sincerely thank them all. Earlier statements of some of the chapter's ideas are in Stokes and Perry (2007) and Perry (1998), and in Perry (2000), Perry, Riege and Brown (1999), and Sobh and Perry (2006).

CHAPTER 4

HOW TO DO (CONVERGENT) INTERVIEWING:
A METHODOLOGY TO START A RESEARCH PROJECT

ABSTRACT

This chapter outlines the relatively new methodology of convergent interviewing that develops a conceptual framework to guide later research. Convergent interviewing involves data analysis after each of about five to ten interviews. First, this chapter describes the essentials of the convergent interviewing methodology, including the two outcomes of a convergent interviewing project, and compares it with other qualitative methods like in-depth interviews, case research and focus groups. Then the methodology's strengths and limitations are noted. The final part shows how the methodology's validity and reliability can be enhanced. The chapter's thesis is that convergent interviewing is more appropriate than some other qualitative methods to investigate under-researched areas because it provides: a way of quickly converging on key issues in the area, an efficient mechanism for data analysis after each interview, and a way of deciding when to stop collecting data.

For acknowledgements and thanks, please refer to the end of this chapter.

INTRODUCTION

Some researchers can find themselves researching an area about which so little is known that they are uncertain how to even begin a research project. Other researchers may be so overwhelmed by previous researchers' articles that they are uncertain about where and how a new contribution can be made. Thus this chapter aims to show how the relatively new, qualitative methodology of convergent interviewing can address issues in these under-researched or confusing areas. Convergent interviewing's key is its data analysis after *each* of a handful of interviews so that a comprehensive picture of interviewees' views is quickly converged on. Thus convergent interviewing's careful analysis of people's views and experience can efficiently and effectively clarify researchers' ideas in the early stage of a research program. This chapter's contribution is a comprehensive treatment of the use of convergent interviewing, closely building on other introductions to convergent interviewing in Carson et al. (2001) and especially Rao and Perry (2003, 2007). This chapter illustrates convergent interviewing with examples from the emerging role of Internet marketing in entrepreneurial enterprises (described in more detail in Rao 2004, Rao & Perry 2003) and from research about investors in Malaysia (Glanville 2009).

The chapter has five parts. First, it describes how to do the convergent interviewing methodology. Then it compares convergent interviewing with other qualitative methods like focus groups. Then convergent interviewing's strengths and limitations are noted. The final part shows how the methodology's validity and reliability can be enhanced.

IMPLEMENTING THE CONVERGENT INTERVIEWING METHODOLOGY

Convergent interviewing is an in-depth interview technique with a structured data analysis process—a technique used to collect, analyse and interpret qualitative information about a person's knowledge, opinions, experiences, attitudes and beliefs from a number of interviews that converge on important issues (Dick 1990; Nair & Riege 1995). That is, the *process* is very structured but the *content* of each interview only gradually becomes more structured—this mix of process and structure allows flexible exploration of the subject matter without determining the answers (Nair & Riege 1995).

In more detail, convergent interviewing is a series of in-depth interviews with knowledgeable people that allow the researcher to refine the questions after *each* interview, to converge on the issues in a topic area. In each interview after the first one, the researchers ask more and more questions about issues raised in previous interviews, to find agreements between the interviewees, or disagreements between them with explanations for those disagreements.

That is, probe questions and new questions about important information are developed after each interview, so that agreements and disagreements among the interviewees are examined in the next interview. The flexibility of convergent interviewing arises out of this continuous refinement of content and process. The interviews stop when stability is reached, that is, when agreement among interviewees is achieved and disagreement among them is explained (by their different industry backgrounds, for example), on all the issues (Nair & Riege 1995). Table 1 shows this process, including the end point of stability on all issues. This section gives more details about how the convergent interviewing method is implemented. It covers four steps: establishing the convergent interview, framing it, closing it, and analysing data. Table 2 summarises these steps.

Table 1 — A diagram of agreements and disagreements about issues in a series of convergent interviews

Issue Interviewee	1	2	3	4	5	6
A	yes	raise	-	-	-	-
B	agree	disagree	raise	raise	-	-
C	agree	disagree	agree	agree	raise	agree
D	agree	disagree	agree	agree	agree	agree

Notes: This diagram is a hypothetical one. In Table 1, interviewee A confirmed one issue (1) suggested in the literature and raised another (2)—new issues are shown as 'raise' in interviewee A's cells. In the next interview, interviewee B agreed about one of these but disagreed with the other. She then raised issues 3 and 4 and so they were probed for agreement or disagreement in later interviews. Note that in the final interview with D, no new issues were raised and so stability had been reached.

Source: Carson et al. (2001)

Table 2 — Framework for the convergent interviews, and their analysis of data

---

Step 1: Establishing the convergent interview
1. The purpose
2. Constructing the interviewer's guide—number and type of questions
3. Selecting and recruiting interviewees
4. Site selection and length of interview
5. Choosing a suitable interviewer

Step 2: Framing the interview
1. Creating a comfortable atmosphere
2. Obtaining informed consent
3. Conducting the interview

Step 3: Closing the convergent interview
Step 4: Analysing and interpreting data of the convergent interviews

---

Source: Adapted from Carson et al. (2001) and Kvale (1996).

Step 1: Establishing the convergent interview
Thoughtful design and planning are essential to conducting interviews (Johnson 2001). In the initial planning stage, the investigators understand their purpose, construct an interview guide, choose interviewees, select the places of the interviews, establish the durations of the interviews, and select the interviewer.

The purpose. The purpose of convergent interviewing is to establish a conceptual framework that will guide data collection in later stages of a research project. That framework is developed in conjunction with the literature, that is, an 'enfolding' approach to the prior theory in the literature (Eisenhardt 1989, p. 25) is used to establish that framework. So, the literature continues to be reviewed while the convergent interviews are being done. In this enfolding process, the researcher begins with a few preliminary propositions and then allows the data and enfolding literature to suggest new directions for shaping the body of knowledge as the interviews proceed. After conducting the first few interviews, new insights lead to a more focused review of the sparse literature.

Constructing the interviewer's guide—number and type of questions. An interviewer's guide defines the issues to be covered and is a loose design for the interviewer to follow (Kvale 1996). The first interviewer's guide contains questions on the broad topics uncovered in the literature review to date. Later interviews have more detailed elements as the interviewees raise further elements. The guide will proceed from broad questions to more specific ones. For example, it could ask about a firm's pricing strategy before asking follow-up questions about how prices are set for particular products. And, for example, it will have specific *probe* sub-questions for many questions, with these probes being about specific aspects of the question. These probes are asked if some aspects were unfortunately not raised by the interviewee when they answered the question. For example, the specific question might be about 'partners' and the probes would be written in the interviewer's guide as '… suppliers?', '… distributors?' and '… customers?'.

The questions in this guide do not have to be asked in the order they are written. With experience, a researcher may be able to get the interviewee involved in a *conversation* rather than a lockstep interview, and the conversation will cover the general topics and associated probe questions without the interviewee necessarily knowing they were planned to be raised. In brief, in a good interview, the questions are often answered before they have to be directly asked (Carson et al. 2001). Techniques to facilitate this conversation are outlined in Step 2 below. After each interview is finished, the emerging structure of the theory is revised and new questions and/or probes are inserted to reflect these new insights before the subsequent interview. That is, later interviews are more structured as the issues crystallise (Dick 1990).

Selecting and recruiting interviewees. When employing a qualitative research methodology, the term 'selecting' respondents can be used in place of the quantitative methodology term of 'sampling' respondents, to help readers to not confuse the two types of research. Nevertheless, sampling was the term used by Patton (2002) and his term, '*purposeful sampling*', is often used to describe how interviewees are selected, so I will continue to use his term of purposeful sampling here, instead of the preferred term of selection.

Purposeful sampling includes many techniques for the selection of interviewees and many studies use its two techniques of opportunistic and typical sampling. Firstly, opportunistic sampling involves following leads that have risen from discussion about the research project with others, possibly from discussion in the course of the researcher's day-to-day work or at conferences. These early discussions and reading can help the convergent interviewer to develop rapport in the later convergent interviews. As well as preventing other potential interview failings, this rapport prevents the interviewees from presenting a sales pitch instead of an account of their management processes—salesmanship is avoided and stewardship found (Bogle 2009). Secondly, typical respondents can be interviewed. These interviewees have practical knowledge of the research problem because they are experienced in the field of research. For example, fund managers can be interviewed in a study of fund management practices.

Another sampling technique is the *snowball* technique and is particularly appropriate when research is concerned with a small, specialised population of people who are knowledgeable about the topics (Neuman 2000; Patton 2002). A part of this sampling process is the careful selection of the first interviewee as the first snowball (Nair & Riege 1995). That is, the first interviewee must be able to direct the researcher to others who are familiar with the area of the research, as well as be an interviewee selected by one of the two techniques above.

Initial contact with potential participants is usually established through email or post, and telephone calls. Where the initial contact is by email or letter, a telephone call is flagged to follow to finalise arrangements (often through the secretary or personal assistant). After being given an overview of the research and the purpose of the interview, the respondents are asked to participate in the interviews. When they agree, the venue and time can be sorted out (Carson et al. 2001).

Number of interviews. The number of interviews in convergent interviewing depends on how many interviews are required to obtain convergence of the underlying research issue (Dick 1990). Research has suggested different sample sizes for the convergent interviewing interviews. Dick (1990) suggested that the sample size should be one percent of a target population of up to 200 and as a minimum the sample size should not be less than 12 people. However, others have argued that sample size is determined when *stability* is reached, that is, when agreement among interviewees is achieved and disagreement among them is explained (by their different industry backgrounds, for example), on all the issues raised, as noted above. For example, Naire & Riege (1995) found stability occurred after only six interviews, and Woodward (1996) found convergence occurred after only five interviews. Overall, stability has been achieved in research projects with about *6 to 10 convergent interviews* (Rao & Perry 2003). The careful selection of interviewees and interview techniques explains this early convergence and why only a small number of interviews is needed. In the Internet research, convergence was achieved after eleven interviews. And in the investor research, stability was reached after five interviews but three more were conducted to make sure that stability had been reached (which confirmed stability had been reached).

Site selection and duration of the interview. Convergent interviews are normally conducted in places that are convenient for both parties and that provide psychological comfort to the interviewee, such as the interviewee's home, the researcher's office or a coffee lounge (Dick 1990). That is, although neutral territory is recommended for conducting convergent interviewing (Dick 1990), familiarity with the respondent and their familiarity with their workplace can facilitate the discussion (Carson et al. 2001). Thus, the respondent is usually asked to choose the time and location of the interview. For example, in the investor research, one respondent asked to be interviewed at a Vietnamese restaurant at lunch time and another was interviewed in the evening at the Royal Selangor Golf Clubhouse. These interviews are conducted face-to-face so that more subtle modes of communication like body language can be read (Gordon & Langmaid 1988), any interviews that are done on the phone should be among the last to be done, so that the interviewer's understanding of what is said can be enhanced by their earlier experience of body language.

In general, each interview takes about 1 to 1.5 hours (Bauer & Gaskell 2000). This time frame can extend when interviewees have a lot of knowledge about the topic. For example, in the investor research, one interviewee had conducted similar reflection and triangulation research when she wrote a book on investing, and another interviewee had two Master's level qualifications, and so both were very interested in the convergent interviewing topic and process and their interviews took more than 1.5 hours.

Choosing a suitable interviewer. A suitable interviewer must know the topic of the research and be an 'active' listener (Carson et al. 2002, p 76). So the interviewer has usually read some literature about the topic and the convergent interviewing processes, and devised the initial interviewer's guide. Making the first interview into a pilot one with a sympathetic colleague who can be phoned up after the interview, helps to fine tune the skills involved.

Step 2: Framing the convergent interview
Framing or setting up the interview is the second step of the interviewing process. There are three aspects involved in framing convergent interviews: creating a comfortable atmosphere, obtaining informed consent and

conducting the interview (Carson et al. 2001). The first aspect in framing a convergent interview is creating a *comfortable atmosphere*. Setting is important here and was covered above. In addition, the interviewer should make the interviewees comfortable and feel free to share their information on the topics in the interviewer's guide that the interviewer is open enough to show them at the beginning. So the interviewer greets the interviewees warmly and then engages a rapport-building informal discussion which lasts about five minutes.

The actual convergent interview begins with obtaining *informed consent*. Interviewing requires researchers to abide by ethical codes of conduct that enforce informed consent (Carson et al. 2001; Warren 2001). In advance of the convergent interviews, an ethics consent form is developed that outlines the research topic and the rights of the interviewees. The interviewees are given the consent form and its salient features are pointed out. The interviewees are then asked to read the form and sign it if they agree with it. Finally, the interviewees are given a personal copy of the consent form.

If the interviewee agrees, the interview is *taped*. Some authorities do not like recording interviews (Wolcott 1990). In contrast, other researchers recommend audio recording because it permits an interviewer to be more attentive to the interviewee and their body language (Carson et al. 2001). Whether permission to tape is given or not, the interviewer should take notes during the interview in an unobtrusive way that does not interrupt the flow of the interview. This note-taking does two things: it helps the interviewer to remember important points, and it lets the speaker know that the interviewer is interested in what they say. And this written record is kept in case of an audio recording malfunction (Carson et al. 2001).

After each convergent interview, the recording is transcribed if time (about five transcription hours per hour of interview) and funds permit; otherwise, the interviewer can just listen to the recording at least once while checking that their notes made during the interview have been adequate. (One way of reducing the time and cost of transcription is to use voice recognition software such as Dragon's. The transcriber (who can be the researcher, of course) must first 'train' the software to recognise their voice. Next, while listening to the taped interview on headphones, the transcriber repeats it word for word into a microphone, that is, 'parrots' it. The software will then convert all the transcriber's words into typescript. With some practice and minor editing, transcriptions can be produced in a fraction of the time usually required (David Launder 2012, pers. comm., 9 December; Nuance 2012).

Conducting the interview. Now the interview can begin. The usual techniques of in-depth interviewing should be used to encourage a quasi-conversation process of covering the questions in the interviewer's guide. These techniques are covered in Carson et al. (2001) and are captured in rules for non-directive interviewing of Armstrong (1985, p. 29):

- *Introduce yourself.* Describe the purpose of the meeting, say why the interviewee was selected, and discuss ethical issues like notes, tape recorders and reports, as noted above. Build rapport by talking about something that you share or something that demonstrates your interest in the interviewee as a person, for example, football scores, the weather. There's nothing devious about the interview process, as illustrated by your showing of your interviewer's guide with its list of questions. You tell the interviewees why you are meeting with them. You are there primarily to listen during this meeting. You want to find out how they view the problem; for example, say, 'Because you are a user of this forest products forecast, I'm interested in finding out what problems you see with it'.
- *Use the funnel technique.* Start with general questions and then go to specific ones later. Your very first question will be a very broad one such as, 'Please tell the story of your marketing management experience.' You will have developed an interviewer's guide that has broad questions that move on to more specific questions.
- *Check your understanding by paraphrasing what they have said.* As the interview proceeds, demonstrate 'active listening' by summarising what you have heard in your own words, to see whether you have correctly understood what has been said (Gordon 1977, p. 55). So ask, for example, 'Is this what you mean …?' Or 'Are you meaning the product has been unexpectedly good?' Or 'So you didn't expect that?'
- *Read their body language.* And possibly show empathy by 'mirroring' their attitudes in your own natural way. For example, if their arms are folded, fold your own in a natural way.
- *Follow up on areas of interest that the interviewee raises.* If the interviewee mentions an area that is of particular interest and you would like to know more, ask! For example, 'You say that you've been having trouble understanding the assumptions behind the forecasts. Could you say more about that?' Again, doing this lets the interviewee know that you are interested in what they say.

- ***Don't evaluate.*** The interviewer should not evaluate what is said. You should avoid positive as well as negative evaluation, for example, there is no need to say, 'That's interesting'. Such evaluations may influence the interviewee to say what will please the interviewer rather than what the interviewee really thinks. The word 'OK' could be about as far as you go in evaluating what the interviewee has said.
- ***Don't interrupt.*** Your job is to listen, so don't stop them talking.
- ***Don't worry about pauses.*** With some practice, you will find that pauses do not bother you; for example, just pretend to be making full notes of what has just been said. Let the interviewee fill the pauses!
- ***Don't introduce your own ideas about the topic.*** Thinking about your own ideas will make it harder for you to listen and will make it difficult for the interviewee to speak.

Consider how the two example convergent interview researchers applied these principles. After some ice breaker questions, a broad question about the interviewees' experience was asked. For example, 'Could you tell me the story about your investment experience?' This broad question helped the respondent share their experience as *they* saw it (Carson et al. 2001). That is, the objective of this opening question was to provide a broad starting point that would lead to further, more specific questions (Nair & Reige 1995) and to define the nature of the topic without implying any constraints on the nature of the response. In addition, this type of 'story' question was designed to not make the respondent anxious about whether they were giving the 'right' answer or not.

Following these topic-entering questions, the interviews started to cover more specific topic questions. During the interviews, the interviewer reminded themselves to not interrupt the respondent, ask leading questions, present their own ideas or be concerned about pauses in the interview (Carson et al. 2001). Interviewees were encouraged to continue talking by showing understanding through active listening. This process kept the interviews focused on the respondent's ideas rather than the interviewer's own (Hollway & Jefferson 2000). *Probing* was used to explore the interviewees' ideas that provided new depth of understanding. Three types of probe questions were used during the interviews: detail-oriented probes (to gain more details on issues being raised), elaborated probes (to get respondents to continue to talk about a topic and keep the interview focused), and clarification probes (to clarify any areas where it is difficult to understand what was said by the respondents) (Maykut & Morehouse 1994; Patton 2002). For example, questions such as 'Can you give me an example of this?' and 'Can you elaborate a little?' were used.

Step 3: Closing the convergent interview
Towards the end of the interview, the interviewer invites a summary of the most important points from the interviewee (Dick 1990). In one of the example research projects, the question to invite summary was 'Of all the issues you have mentioned, what are the most and least important issues?' and then questions were asked about the priority of the issues such as 'Could you please prioritise them in order of importance?' (Rao & Perry 2007). Next, interviewees were asked to comment on the interviewer's initial conceptual framework that was driving the research project at that time.

Then the interviewer used several non-verbal cues to indicate the interview was coming to an end. For example, they turned off the recording device and sat back. They then asked the interviewees if they had any final questions or issues they wanted to raise, and they highlighted the fact that interviewees in the report would be disguised. Once all these tasks had been done, the interviewer thanked the interviewees for their contribution and their time, and left the interview site. By the way, the very last things that interviewees say—after the tape recorder and the notes have been put away—are sometimes quite insightful.

Step 4: Analysing and interpreting data of the convergent interviews
After each interview, the tape and notes are checked and a transcription possibly made, as explained in step 2 above. A summary note of the issues raised is also drawn up as soon as possible. These notes contain two parts: the issues and an interpretation of those issues. Previous interpretations of the issues are revised until ambiguities are resolved and key points are identified (Dick 1990). This data analysis after each interview follows the five phases of data analysis described in detail in step 6 of this book's Chapter 3 about case research: familiarisation, coding, developing themes in the coded data, establishing major themes, and reporting.

Thus the penultimate outcome of the convergent interviewing process is a list of *major themes* that were progressively raised and investigated in the interviews, along the lines of the example in Table 3.

This table is constructed by progressive content analysis of the interview transcripts and usually fits the themes into three to five 'chunks' of ideas called research issues. The table shows how the number of issues involved in the topic area increased as each interviewee in turn added their insights to what had been said before, until the final interview added no new issues, that is, there are no empty cells in the last two rows. Both agreements between interviewees and disagreements that could be explained are in the table. For example, some of the entries in an Internet research table about the third research issue uncovered in the interviews encompassed points like:

Research Issue 3: Internet usage is perceived to be positively associated with business performance.
- The use of the Internet has a positive effect on sales and market share.
- The use of the Internet has a positive effect on long-term profits but not on short term profits.
- The use of the Internet has a positive effect on return on assets.

How the table and the data analysis appeared in the final detailed report are in Table 3 (from Rao 2002).

Table 3 — Excerpts from the data analysis of the Internet convergent interviewing research

5. Research issue 3: Determinants of relational outcomes of business performance and/or propensity to stay											
• Difficulty in measuring Internet's effect on business performance	*	√	√	√	√	√	√	√	√	√	√
• The use of the Internet has little effect on sales and market share	*	*	√	x	√	√	√	x	√	√	√
• The use of the Internet has little effect on short-term profit level	*	*	√	x	√	√	√	√	√	√	√
• The use of the Internet has a positive effect on long-term profit level	*	√	√	x	√	x	√	√	√	x	√
• The use of the Internet has little effect on return on assets	*	√	√	√	√	√	√	√	√	√	√
• Intention to stay in the Internet relationship	*	*	√	√	√	x	x	√	√	√	√

Source: Rao (2002).

Determinants of relational outcomes of business performance and/or propensity to stay in an Internet-facilitated relationship. *All interviewees agreed that improved business performance is still the goal they are trying to achieve from establishing and developing exchange relationships in an Internet environment. 'It is critical…it is the bottom line of any business relationship…it (profitability) is the criteria to choose potential clients to do business with' (D). With the Internet, the expectation of their exchange partners' performance is higher and is seen as a continually improving process. Overall, Internet use is perceived to have a positive effect on business performance. That is, it facilitates business performance although it is not the main component of the business performance. For example, 'the Internet has a somewhat* *secondary influence on our business performance...it definitely helps us to deliver service'* (C). *'The Internet is only part of the marketing mix'* (H).

However, the extent to which the Internet can assist in different aspects of business performance is difficult to measure, as shown in block 5 in Table 3. Some interviewees were able to discuss the effect of Internet use specifically from a sales and market share perspective. *'Providing our goods and services online definitely assists with sales'* (B). Others simply did not use business performance as a criterion for measuring because it is difficult to monitor.

Further, interviewees' opinions about the effect on profit level differed again. Most of them stated that Internet usage has little effect on their short-term profit level but they have the expectation of an increased long-term profit level. For example, *'We have expectations for long-term profit. That is the justification to what we are doing (using the Internet) now'* (I). *'...there is a lag time from the time we started and the time we are actually making money from it'* (E). *'A lot of long-term, ongoing support is coming through the Internet, so return on assets is ongoing and long-term as well'* (H). *'My personal expectation on return on assets is high. It comes from greatly reduced costs, reduced handling, increased automation, extended market reach and so on'* (B). *'We will have to get the efficiency out of it over a longer period of time'* (C).

Moreover, all interviewees expressed their intention to stay in Internet-facilitated relationships and agreed that Internet use is blended into their long-term, strategic planning. *'The Internet will not change everything automatically. But it makes you look at your business differently and see what sort of opportunities it can bring to you. A business plan is critical in achieving that'* (B). In addition, it seems propensity to stay is the most appropriate construct amongst all the constructs explored given that most interviewees indicated the difficulty in giving information regarding their profitability, market share or business performance.

In brief, a wider number of viewpoints was presented amongst interviewees about how Internet use has impacted on business performance, confirming that the choice of propensity to stay in the relationship that has been justified in Section 2.4 is more appropriate than business performance in this Internet-facilitated relationship marketing research.

A table and analysis like Table 3 is the initial outcome of convergent interviewing but it should be a stepping-stone towards another outcome— a *conceptual framework*. That is, from a close examination of the quotations about the issues summarised in the table and its analysis, and from the scant literature, a new conceptual framework about the research project's objectives can be developed. This stepping from a first, exploratory outcome to a final outcome is common in qualitative research (Miles & Huberman 1994). Note that *early* versions of a model of this framework were presented to the interviewees at the end of each interview, for their comments and ideas about revisions.

In our experience, a comprehensive conceptual model can rarely be developed before the convergent interviews begin because there is so little previous research about the variables involved and, in particular, the complex interrelationships among the variables cannot be unearthed without the flexible, in-depth processes of convergent interviewing. Incidentally, after a model is finalised, some researchers have used qualitative case research in the second stage of a research project.

However, the Internet research project moved directly to a survey's *statistical* generalisation because several of the variables identified in the convergent interviews had already been investigated in previous research. That is, it used structural equation modelling of survey data to test the conceptual model developed in stage 1. Most of the model's variables and relationships were shown to be valid.

A COMPARISON OF CONVERGENT INTERVIEWING WITH ALTERNATIVE METHODOLOGIES

Now, how does the convergent interviewing methodology compare with some alternative qualitative methodologies? In early stages of theory building, little is known about the topic area and several qualitative methods may be used to refine research issues and reduce uncertainty about a research topic. This section compares convergent interviewing with the more often used methods of in-depth interview, case research and focus groups, to explain why convergent interviewing should be chosen in a theory-building research project. The major characteristics of and differences between convergent interviews, in-depth interviews, case research and focus group studies are illustrated in Table 4 and form the basis for this discussion (Rao & Perry 2007). Essentially, convergent interviewing is more appropriate for the early stage of many research projects than the other methods because it provides:

- a way of quickly converging on key issues in an emerging area
- an efficient mechanism for data analysis after each interview
- a way of deciding when to stop collecting data.

Table 4 — Differences between convergent interviews, in-depth interviews and case research

Qualitative method / Characteristics	In-depth interviews	Convergent interviews	Case research	Focus groups
1. Main objective	To obtain rich and detailed information	Narrow down research focus	Mainly theory building/ confirming	Group interaction
2. Level of prior theory requirement	Low	Low	Medium to high	To obtain insights and various ideas
3. Process	Flexible—unstructured to structured	Structured process with continuous refinement	Structured and standard procedures	Flexible—unstructured to structured
4. Content	Unstructured to structured	Unstructured	Somewhat structured	Unstructured
5. Strengths	Replication	Progressive	Replication	Synergistic effect in a group setting
6. Weaknesses	Results may be biased and are not for theory testing	Potential interviewer bias, requirement of interviewer's knowledge and not sufficient on its own	Requirement of sufficient prior theory	Conforming effects in a group setting

Source: developed from Carson et al. (2001) and Yin (2009).

In-depth interview vs convergent interview. Begin with a comparison of standard in-depth interviewing with convergent interviewing. In-depth interviews are not as useful as convergent interviewing because convergent interviewing has a more structured way of processing interviews and analysing data. Traditional in-depth interviews are analysed once at the end of all of them. But the advantage of convergent interviewing over in-depth interviewing lies in its already noted progression over several interviews that enables the research to refine content and process of the interview continuously to narrow down broad research issues (Dick 1990) into more focused ones at the end of the research program. As well, convergent interviewing provides an ending point where stability is achieved. These advantages of convergent interviewing over other interviewing methods of progressive exploration and data analysis, and the identification of an ending point, are also advantages over the other methods to be discussed next.

Case research vs convergent interview. The case research method is not as useful as convergent interviewing in the early stage of a research project because there is often insufficient prior theory about the research problem to use case research. Admittedly, case research can be used to investigate a new research area or contemporary phenomenon within a dynamically changing, real life context (Yin 2009; Carson et al. 2001). However, many researchers emphasise the importance of entering all qualitative research with *some* initial theory or 'pre-structure' (Miles & Huberman 1984, p. 17; Yin 2009). This pre-structure gained in convergent interviewing will be needed to develop the many questions for a case research interviewer's guide (that have to be the same across all the interviews in case research). That is, a mix of induction and deduction may be required for a research program involving case research (Perry 2001), with the early stages being more induction then deduction. This blending of induction and deduction can be achieved by incorporating convergent interviews in the first stage of a project to provide the prior theory for the development of the interviewer's guide in the second, case research stage.

Focus groups vs convergent interviews. Finally, focus groups may not be appropriate in the first stages of a research project because of the type of data that a first stage aims at obtaining. Focus groups are appropriate when research needs to use group interaction to produce data and insights that would be less accessible without the interaction within a group (Morgan 1993). That is, focus groups are most useful and appropriate in exploratory and developmental phases of a research where little is known about a somewhat subjective phenomenon (Morgan & Krueger 1993). However, the information for many research projects can be obtained without the synergistic effect of a group setting offered by focus groups (Morgan 1993). Indeed, business people in a focus group are unlikely to divulge their business innovations to others within the group who might be their competitors.

In brief, convergent interviewing is an appropriate methodology for the first stage of many research projects.

STRENGTHS AND LIMITATIONS OF THE CONVERGENT INTERVIEWING TECHNIQUE

From the description above, convergent interviewing offers three main strengths. Firstly, convergent interviewing is useful for the exploration of areas lacking an established theoretical base. That is, the flexibility provided by the convergent interviewing method allows for the refinement of research issues throughout the course of the interviews, resulting in the consolidation of the existing body of knowledge and a more precisely defined research problem (Dick 1990). Secondly, it provides a flexible instrument to allow all issues related to the research problem to be identified and explored. This flexibility of convergent interviewing allows researchers to use a funnelling process in which they control the flow of the type of information being sought (Riege 2003).

The final strength of convergent interviewing is that the subjectivity inherent in qualitative data is largely overcome by the interviewer attempting to always explain answers after each interview, that is, to 'disprove the emerging explanation of the data' (Dick 1990, p. 11). That is, subjective data is refined through the use of convergence and divergence that adds relatively 'objective' methods to the refinement of subjective data (Dick 1990).

Despite these strengths, there are limitations associated with the convergent interviewing technique. Firstly, convergent interviewing may allow interviewer bias to occur (Dick 1990), like most qualitative methods. To guard against this bias, the interviewers need to be not only skilful and experienced, but also have some knowledge about the subject matter and be able to maintain data quality when recording and analysing the data obtained from the interviews. For instance, in one of the example research projects, the researcher had previous qualitative research training, and had begun to review the literature about broader literatures of Internet marketing and relationship marketing (Rao & Perry 2007).

Secondly, the convergent interviewing method requires the interviewee to be knowledgeable about the research subject matter and so be able to contribute meaningful information to the exploratory research. In one of the example research projects, the researcher used the snowballing technique to access practitioner experts about the Internet who could provide their information and experience about the research topic (Rao & Perry 2007).

After each interview, the interviewee was sufficiently familiar with the aims and topics of the research to refer the researcher to other experts. It is advisable to ask each interviewee for more than one other expert, at the end of an interview, to reduce the chances of a snowballing research project being locked into a mindset of just one network of experts. For example, probe an interviewee for experts from other industries or for experts that the interviewee has rarely interacted with or not met.

The final limitation of the convergent interviewing methodology is that it is sometimes not sufficient on its own to provide results that can be generalised to a wider population (Marshall & Rossman 1995; Maykut & Morehouse 1994). However, this limitation was overcome in the example Internet and other research projects because the aim was merely to build a theory for *later* testing; indeed, quantitative research was used later in the Internet project to validate the theory building stage of convergent interviewing (Rao 2004).

On balance, then, the strengths of convergent interviewing outweigh its limitations.

ESTABLISHING THE VALIDITY AND RELIABILITY OF THE CONVERGENT INTERVIEWING RESEARCH

This final section examines the issues of achieving validity and reliability in convergent interviews (Riege 2003). Validity and reliability in qualitative research can be achieved through forms of cross-checking. These in-built checks and controls for qualitative research can be summarised under four common tests of research design, namely, construct validity, internal validity, external validity and reliability (Yin 2009) and are summarised in Table 5.

Table 5 — Tests for validity and reliability of qualitative research such as convergent interviewing

TEST	RESEARCH DESIGN	PHASE OF RESEARCH
Construct validity	• data collected from multiple sources (convergent interviews) provide multiple measures of the same phenomenon	research design and data analysis
	• establishment of triangulation of interview questions	research design and data analysis
	• in-built negative case analysis	data analysis
	• flexibility of the proposed theoretical framework	research design and data collection
Internal validity	• sample selection for information richness	research design
External validity	• sample selection for theoretical replication	research design
Reliability	• interview guide developed for the collection of data	data collection and analysis
	• structured process for administration and interpretation of convergent interviews	data collection
	• use of a steering committee	research design data collection and analysis

Source: developed from Yin (2009).

Construct validity refers to the formation of suitable operational measures for the concepts being investigated (Zikmund 2000). Convergent interviewing achieves construct validity through three tactics. Firstly, triangulation of interview questions is established in the research design stage through two or more carefully worded questions that looked at constructs from different angles. Secondly, the convergent interview method contains an in-built negative case analysis where, in each interview and before the next, the technique explicitly requires that the interviewer attempt to disprove emerging explanations interpreted in the data (Dick 1990). Finally, the flexibility of the mode allows the interviewer to re-evaluate and re-design both the content and process of the interview program, thus establishing content validity.

Internal validity refers to causal relationships and the validity of the influence of one variable on other variables (Zikmund 2000). Internal validity in the convergent interviews is achieved through purposeful sample selection on the basis of 'information richness' (Patton 1990, p. 181), and is described in some detail below.

External validity concerns the ability of the research findings to be generalised beyond the immediate study (Sekaran 2000). In convergent interviewing, some external validity can be achieved through theoretical replication in the interviewee selection described below. That is, experts are selected to ensure that a cross-section of opinions was provided.

Reliability refers to how consistently a technique measures the concepts it is supposed to measure, enabling other researchers to repeat the study and attain similar findings (Sekaran 2000). Convergent interviewing secures reliability through five tactics. Firstly, reliability is attained through the structured process of convergent interviews. Secondly, reliability is achieved through organizing a structured process for recording, writing and interpreting data.

A third reliability procedure is to have at least two interviewers conduct the interviews, working individually but in parallel with each other (Dick 1990). In addition, research reliability is achieved through comparing this research's findings with those of other, albeit few, researchers in the literature. Finally, the use of a steering committee to assist in the design and administration of the interview program is another way that reliability can be achieved (Guba & Lincoln 1994). If a number of the members of the committee agree about a phenomenon, then their collective judgment is relatively objective.

In brief, four tests of validity and reliability can be applied to the first, qualitative stage of a research project.

CONCLUSION

In summary, this chapter provided a comprehensive description of the convergent interviewing method, compared convergent interviewing with other qualitative methods, showed how its validity and reliability can be enhanced, reviewed its strengths and limitations and finally noted how it can be implemented.

In conclusion, convergent interviewing is more appropriate than in-depth interviews, case research and focus groups in under-researched areas where there are only a few experts. It provides a way of quickly converging on key issues in the area, has an efficient mechanism for data analysis after each interview, and has a way of deciding when to stop collecting data. It is often an ideal way to begin a research project.

ACKNOWLEDGMENTS

This chapter is closely based on and even incorporates some parts of reports by Rao & Perry (2003, 2007), Rao (2002), Carson et al. (2001) and Glanville (2009) in particular. Its foundations are in the psychology book by convergent interviewing's developer, Bob Dick (1990) and incorporates ideas and words of reports by several others who have refined the process for marketing research, for example, Drs Gerry Batonda, Godwin Nair, Andi Riege and Tracy Woodward. I thank and acknowledge all of them for their pioneering work.

CHAPTER 5

HOW TO DO ACTION RESEARCH AND REPORT IT FOR AN ACADEMIC AUDIENCE

ABSTRACT

Although many papers and books have been written about conducting an action research project to manage change in one particular situation, it is difficult for academic researchers to generate understandings that can be applied outside the particular situation of an action research project. This chapter aims to assist generation of those understandings by distinguishing the scientific paradigms underlying action research and other management research, focussing on the critical theory and realism paradigms involved in them. Because the paradigms are so different, a two-'project' approach to using action research in management research is developed. One project is based on the customary action research cycles, and the other project is based on the stages of an academic research project like a journal article or a thesis. How to integrate and implement the two projects is detailed, together with an analysis of the quality criteria of the two projects. Examples are provided.

For acknowledgements and thanks, please refer to the end of this chapter.

INTRODUCTION

Multiple methods research combines qualitative and quantitative methods like a focus group and a survey. But using multiple methods is difficult because the two methods look at different phenomena. The research problem of qualitative research is usually a 'how and/or why' problem, while the research problem of quantitative research is usually a 'what' problem. A multiple methods researcher cannot triangulate upon a single phenomenon when different social realities are being investigated. For example, quantitative research could uncover the inputs and outputs of a phenomenon but cannot provide the understanding that explains *how* they operate in particular contexts (Silverman 2008). These difficulties in using multiple methods arise because the different methods operate within different scientific paradigms (Green & Caracelli 2003). An example of this paradigmatic difficulty occurs when the results of an action research project in one situation have to be generalised to other situations.

The action research method spirals through a four-step process of planning, acting, observing and reflecting on results generated from a particular project or body of work (Zuber-Skerritt & Perry 2000; Dick 2000). Essentially, the method is used by a group of people who work together to improve their work processes, that is, a community of practitioners or co-researchers (Alrichter et. al. 2000; Reason & Bradbury 2008). So, action research is process-oriented in one work situation that is *changing*. It looks at action to bring about change of one workgroup's processes, by adding to the workgroup's understanding of those processes. Throughout, action research is collaborative, problem-focused, context-specific, future-oriented, and integrates thought and action in an emerging way. It allows practitioners to research their own professional activities by critically examining their own beliefs and practices over time. So, for example, it helps managers to be multidisciplinary and work across technical, cultural and functional boundaries to improve practice at the workplace. Action research is described later in this chapter.

But an action research project commonly involves just *one* organisation—it is 'insider' research about one situation, rather than 'outsider' research that develops understanding that can be generalised to many other organisations (McNiff & Whitehead 2010, p. 19). As an extension of this insider form of action research to other situations, the use of two related but distinct views about research 'projects' has been established for graduate management programs—the core action research project and the *generalising* research project (Perry & Zuber-Skerritt 1992; Zuber-Skerrit & Perry 2002). Using these two views of a 'project' allows a researcher to think about the two audiences of reports about action research. The first audience is the stakeholders within one *particular* organisation such as the core action research project's sponsor. The second audience are more interested in analytic generalisation (Yin 2009); these second academics want to build a theory about a phenomenon from that particular organisation to *other* organisations. That is, the readers of the first report will be a community of practitioners. The readers of the second report will usually be a community of academic researchers but they could also be marketing consultants facing a similar sort of problem across several clients. In other words, an action research project may enhance learning by managers and others within an organisation, but how can it also make a contribution to a body of knowledge that interests academics?

That is, an action researcher/social scientist faces two goals or 'imperatives' (McKay & Marshall 2001, p. 46). One goal is to solve a practical problem within an organisation, and the second is to generate new knowledge and understanding. How to address both these goals has rarely been addressed in the literature (Perry & Zuber-Skerritt 1994; Carson et al. 2001) and there is 'little direct guidance on "how to do" it' (McKay & Marshall 2001, p. 49). For example, one university academic dismissed action research for creating knowledge with: 'If you want to do research, do research; if you want to organize, then go do action research' (Herr & Anderson 2005, p. xii). Moreover, the concept of two different sets of stakeholders for action research has rarely been extended in the action research literature to consider the *paradigms* or worldviews of both these stakeholders, and little study has been done about those paradigms' influence upon judging the quality of those action research projects, for example, their validity and reliability (Thompson & Perry 2004). Authors who do address this issue of two stakeholders are Herr and Anderson (2005) and Dick (n.d.), but they essentially remain within the usual action research paradigm; readers who do not want to switch paradigms to increase their influence in academic journals can consider authors like those.

Thus the aim of this chapter is to identify the scientific paradigms appropriate for each of two research 'projects'—the 'core' action research project and the 'generalising' research project—and to identify the criteria that could be used in each project to judge its quality (the chapter is closely based on Perry 2000, Thompson & Perry 2004; Zuber-Skerrit & Perry 2002). Essentially, the chapter argues that the critical theory paradigm is appropriate for the first, core action research project and the realism paradigm is appropriate for the second, generalising research project. Quality criteria from these two paradigms could be used to judge how well each is done. Our contributions for action researchers are identifying the two paradigms for these purposes, and the illustrations of using their quality criteria. These contributions are important because they provide improved, deep understanding of both practical and academic research processes.

The chapter has two parts. First, the paradigms are introduced and evaluated. Then, the 'core' action research project and the 'generalising' research project are described and examples presented. Quality of the two projects finishes the chapter.

FOUR PARADIGMS

A fourfold classification of scientific paradigms is: positivism, critical theory, constructivism and realism (based on Guba & Lincoln 2005; Perry, Riege & Brown 1999; Perry 2000), and they are summarised in Table 1. Each paradigm is appropriate for different approaches to different phenomena. Chapter 3 of this book has a complete discussion of these four paradigms; that chapter's treatment focussed on realism's appropriateness for the case research methodology, but this chapter focusses on both critical theory's appropriateness for the action research methodology and how an academic's realism has to be blended onto an action research project.

Positivism. The first, positivism paradigm is the most widely used paradigm for business school research and assumes implicitly or explicitly that reality can be measured by viewing it through a one way, value-free mirror. Its assumptions are summarised in the left-hand column of Table 1. These assumptions are used by engineers, for example, to research a physical science phenomenon like a bridge. But should they be used by social scientists like management researchers?

Table 1 — Four scientific paradigms

ELEMENT	PARADIGM			
	Positivism	Constructivism	Critical theory	Realism
Ontology	reality is real and apprehensible	multiple local and specific 'constructed' realities	'virtual' reality shaped by social, economic, ethnic, political, cultural, and gender values, crystallised over time	reality is 'real' but only imperfectly and probabilistically apprehensible and so triangulation from many sources is required to try to know it

Table 1 — Four scientific paradigms (contd)

ELEMENT	PARADIGM			
	Positivism	Constructivism	Critical theory	Realism
Epistemology	findings true—researcher is objective by viewing reality through a 'one-way mirror'	created findings—researcher is a 'passionate participant' within the world being investigated	value mediated findings—researcher is a 'transformative intellectual' who changes the social world within which participants live	findings probably true—researcher is value-aware and needs to triangulate any perceptions he or she is collecting
Common methodologies	Mostly concerns with a testing of theory. Thus mainly quantitative methods such as: survey, experiments, and verification of hypotheses	In-depth unstructured interviews, participant observation, action research, and grounded theory research	Action research and participant observation	Mainly qualitative methods such as case studies and convergent interviews

Note: Essentially, ontology is 'reality', epistemology is the relationship between that reality and the researcher and methodology is the technique used by the researcher to discover that reality.

Source: based on Perry, Riege and Brown (1999), which itself was based on Guba and Lincoln (1994) from where the quotations come.

These positivism assumptions are prevalent in business school research and are almost its 'default' assumptions. But the assumptions are inappropriate for researching social science phenomena like management, marketing and other professional phenomena. For an example of their inappropriateness, consider that replications do not usually produce the same results as prior research, as one would expect in positivism research. Only 15 percent of replication studies in the social science of marketing fully confirmed the prior findings and only 25 percent partially confirmed them (Hubbard & Armstrong 1994). Indeed, of those few replication studies that supported prior research, over half were done by the *same* researcher as did the prior research (Hubbard & Vetter 1996), suggesting that the research was not done in the value-free way that positivism supposes. Clearly, some phenomena in the social sciences cannot be approached through positivism research—they are not positivism's easily apprehended phenomena and the researcher is not a value-free observer.

Thus it should not be surprising that real world managers consider most academic research coming out of positivism-based business schools is irrelevant, as noted in this book's Chapter 3. Even some academic researchers are realizing this fact, as shown in this summary of the many findings that demonstrate business schools' academic 'rigor' has overshadowed relevance:

> For almost 2 decades, scholars themselves have been expressing concerns that an excessive preoccupation with theory might bind business school research into a "straightjacket" that limits its relevance and value to practice (e.g., Bettis, 1991; Daft & Lewin, 1990). However, these criticisms now seem to be reaching an almost feverish pitch, with many prominent scholars suggesting that research has *overemphasized rigor* (e.g., following the scientific method) and theory (Hambrick, 2007) at the expense of *relevance and value to practice* (Bartunek, 2007; Hambrick, 2007; McGrath, 2007; Pfeffer, 2007; Tsui, 2007). To make matters worse, such research may be guiding what faculty teach in the classroom (Rubin & Dierdorff, 2009), and according to Ghoshal (2005), may *actually negatively influence practice* (O'Brien et al. 2010, p. 638; emphases added).

In brief, I argue that using positivism as the default paradigm in social sciences like management and marketing is a garden path that leads nowhere in particular. This chapter will not return to the positivism paradigm.

Constructivism and critical theory. Two alternatives to positivism in the social sciences can be categorised within the two paradigms of constructivism and critical theory. The two paradigms are summarised in the middle columns of Table 1. Essentially, these paradigms argue that the world is 'constructed' by individuals in constructivism and by groups in critical theory. These paradigms investigate important phenomena.

For example, some people perceive Levi jeans are the best jeans and worth buying, even though tests done within a positivism framework by consumer magazines show their cloth, stitching and buttoning is not as well-constructed as other brands' jeans. Similarly, a person can commit suicide because they perceive themselves to be in a black, depressing world, whether that external world is 'really' as bad as they perceive it to be or not. That is, a core element of these two paradigms is that each person's or group's constructed reality is so powerful an influence on their behaviour that any external reality is relatively unimportant. In brief, these two paradigms can sometime explain certain phenomena like brand loyalty.

In these two paradigms, there is no way of comparing the multiple constructed realities of different people or groups. However, this incommensurability of perceptions, that is, the *relativism* at the heart of these paradigms, makes the two paradigms a *cul de sac* for many academic researchers. For example, Hunt (1991) asks how these paradigms can help in trying to research whether the Holocaust occurred to Jews in the 1940s—some people perceive that it occurred and some that it did not, and these differences cannot be compared within the two paradigms of constructivism and critical theory:

> It is indeed true that one of the 'multiple realities' that some people hold… is that the Holocaust never occurred … An alternative 'multiple reality' is that the Holocaust did in fact occur … Which 'multiple reality' is correct? Sincere … advocates of reality relativism must stand mute when confronted with this question.

One way offered out of this *cul de sac* is negotiations between people with differently constructed worlds, to arrive at some shared understanding (Guba & Lincoln 2005). But will these negotiations be possible when the people have unequal power? For example, will burglars who perceive that stealing possessions away from wealthier people is equitable, and wealthy householders who do not want their homes burgled, be able to negotiate some shared understanding? The answer must be a clear 'No':

> it is hard not to snigger when Guba and Lincoln talk about getting stakeholders to agree to and formally sign 'conditions for a productive hermeneutic dialectic'… [Their] hermeneutic dialectic circles (not surprisingly) go round in circles, rather than constituting a linear advance on truth. (Pawson and Tilley 1997, pp. 16-21)

Moreover, constructivism and critical theory are not especially relevant in research about an organisation having to survive within a market, because marketing managers have to deal with a world that is external, that is *out there* and that does not particularly care about the perceptions of an individual manager:

> In marketing, the company's *external* environment is always more important than the internal. The real decisions are made in the world outside—among consumers, middlemen, competitors, politicians, legislators and trade organisations. The external environment is neither particularly knowledgeable nor interested in the company and its development. (Gummesson 2000, p. 105; italics added)

In brief, subjective 'meaning' within constructed realities may indeed determine some outcomes like customers' choice of jeans but not issues concerning the management of those perceptions. So constructivism and critical theory may be appropriate paradigms for research about important social science phenomena like suicide, falling in love, family life, office power politics in big organisations with slow or blurry feedback loops to the outside, political ideologies, racism and nationalism. But many academic researchers are interested in a school of thought about other phenomena than these, across many situations that do need to be compared.

Critical theory is the paradigm that underlies *action research* within groups, as described in the next section of this chapter. But while critical theory is the paradigm of action researchers investigating one particular workgroup, it is a *cul de sac* for much management research such as research about management. My aim here is to establish how action research within the critical theory paradigm can be made relevant to social scientists working in another paradigm.

Realism. We sometimes need to move away from the paradigms above and into the paradigm of realism. This realism view of the world consists of abstract things that are born of people's minds but exist independently of any one person … it is 'largely autonomous, though created by us' (Magee 1985, p. 61). That world could be a country's legal system or the body of academic knowledge about leadership or market segmentation, for example. A person's perceptions are a window on to that blurry, external reality. Realism is summarised in the right-hand column of Table 1 and is about mechanisms of structures within a social context that *do* exist 'out there' (Pawson & Tilley 1997). That world of mechanisms and their contexts is not as straightforward as the world that physical scientists like engineers work within. An engineer knows that too much weight upon a bridge will definitely cause the bridge to fall. But social science realists work with causal *tendencies* rather than causal certainties—A may cause B sometimes but not always or even mostly. For example, whether lights at a carpark will cause car thefts to decrease may depend upon the hours that the carpark is used and its location. In other words, sometimes the lights will reduce crime and sometimes they may not, depending on the context. Similarly, whether a marketing communication tactic is successful will depend upon many contextual conditions like competitor's reactions. The imprecision of these causal tendencies is exacerbated by the ability of people to change their behaviour after reflecting upon it.

This realism paradigm is the worldview of many social scientists investigating many workgroups, and covers a wider canvas than the single workgroup focus of an action researcher working within the critical theory paradigm. How can the two paradigms be bridged?

ACTION RESEARCH IS A BLEND OF TWO PARADIGMS

Upon this foundation of paradigms, consider how an academic action researcher has to somehow blend the critical theory and the realism paradigms. Essentially, action research can be a way of conducting research within an organisation that benefits both the organisation and the body of knowledge about which readers of an academic journal article or thesis are interested. This section will firstly cover a definition of normal, 'pure' action research for managers and consultants that show it is process-oriented, emancipatory and does not bother with generalisation beyond the context. Then it will show how an academic's research can be divided into a core action research project and into a generalising project that provides action research results for academics.

Core action research. Before discussing action research, we need to clarify what it is. In its purest form, action research emphasises three key aspects (Zuber-Skerritt 2001):

- a group of people at work together
- involved in the cycle of planning, acting, observing and reflecting on their work as shown in Figure 1, more deliberately and systematically than usual
- a public report of that experience (such as a report to an organisation's board).

That is, action research is process-oriented in one work situation. It looks at action to bring about change of one workgroup's processes, and also at adding to the workgroup's understanding of those processes. Therefore change and learning are its two outcomes.

Figure 1 — *The spiral of action research cycles*

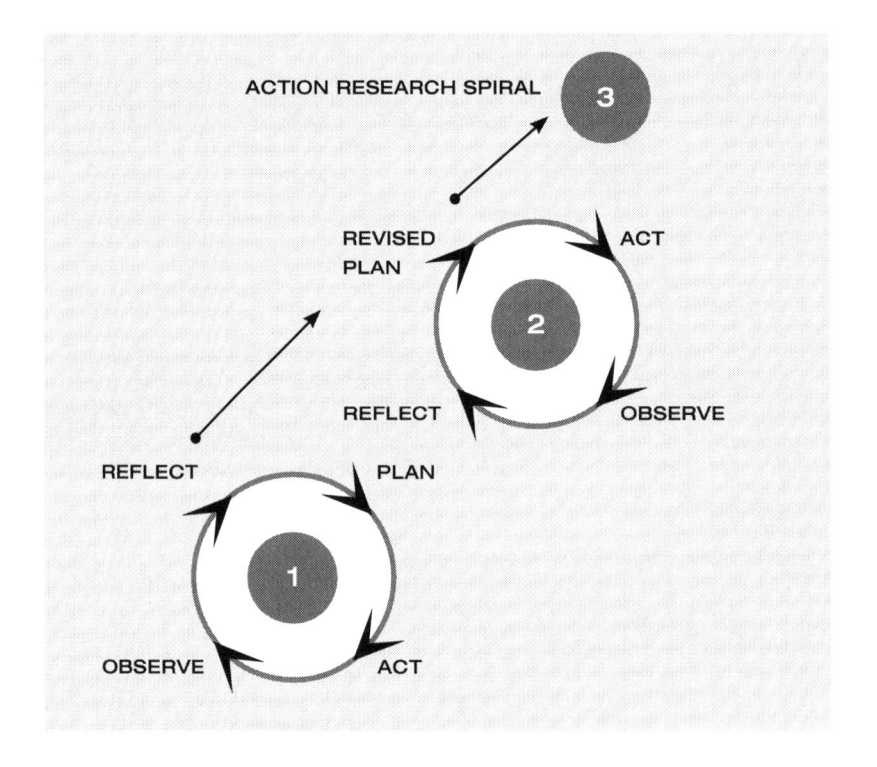

Source: Zuber-Skerritt (2001, p. 15).

This definition highlights the critical theory paradigm underlying action research by noting that it involves a group of people who are transforming how they construct their perceived work 'reality'. The action researchers' cycles in Figure 1 may be testing out their perceptions of an outside reality, but the *emphasis* is on the group's *perceptions* because they drive behaviour within one organisation.

Sources of data. The data collected in each of these cycles can be of two types. Secondary data can be managers' plans and reports or students' assignments, newsletters, checklists, videos and photographs. And primary data can be collected from the action research group or from others in the organisation, including interview notes and transcripts, results of surveys of the group or of others in the organisation, and findings of focus groups. Of course, the most critical primary data are the agendas and minutes of group meetings, the public report of the group's experience and the journal of the researcher. That journal should record: the researcher's emerging understandings; changes in methods and conclusions about them; the literature read and any confirmations or disconfirmations it provides; and some quotations from the group or other people (Dick 1997). By the way, because meetings are important in action research, researchers are advised to become skilled in managing meetings (for example, Appendix 1 of Thompson 2004).

Examples. Several examples of core action research projects are in Abraham (2012). Another example of a core action research project involved key members of a consulting group bidding to run a government-funded, development aid project (Thompson 2003). It began with a 'pre-step' of *reconnaissance* about the research project's context and purpose before the first planning phase (Coghlan & Brannick 2010, p. 8). The reconnaissance involved reading the literature about project management, development aid and cross-cultural management, and then involved interviews with four outside experts to examine the external reality built by the perceptions of others and how the real world problem could possibly be addressed. Discussions and informal interviews were also held with management and other staff.

That reconnaissance pre-step was the base for the **planning** phase of the first action research cycle, and involved assessing the parameters of the bidding problem and the strategy for addressing that problem. The second phase of the first action research cycle was **implementation** of the plan, that is, development of the bid documents. During the next **observe** phase, the researcher collected data from the sources noted above. Then **reflection** was carried out in meetings of the group organised by the researcher, and included evaluation of what had happened during the implementation stage that included submission of the (unsuccessful) application for the government grant. The reflection phase marked the end of the first cycle and led to the beginning of a new cycle about bidding on a second grant. In all the four phases, the researcher collected data from the secondary and primary sources noted above.

After the second cycle, the researcher switched from his critical theory paradigm, and started operating in the realism paradigm while he concentrated on his thesis writing.

Another example of core action research is James' project. He was a human resource manager in a large government body which was introducing a new information system in a project involving contracted information systems consultants. He arranged 1½ hour meetings each fortnight for three other public servants who were also involved in the project, and two consultants. He facilitated the meetings and focused the reflection discussion on the processes they were using in the project. They wrote a report of their deliberations for the body's senior management with conclusions about the IT system introduction.

These core action research projects fit within the critical theory paradigm, that is, they are based on perceptions bound by their *relativism*. In contrast, most managers and academics are results-oriented to an external world. Moreover, 'pure' action research is ideally 'emancipatory' where all members of the workgroup have equal responsibility for the outcomes, as shown in Table 2. However, management situations are usually 'technical' or 'practical' (using the terms in Table 2) because of different levels of responsibility for budget outcomes among group members. In other words, pure action research may be rare in management situations. Finally, pure action research virtually ignores analytic generalisation, that is, how the findings from one situation can be applied in other situations or firms or industries (Yin 2009). It is this generalisation that readers of academic articles and theses are interested in, explaining why one of the most common criticisms of published action research is that 'it lacks theory' (Coghlan & Brannick 2010, p. 115). Thus critical theory paradigm research is marginal among academics (Guba & Lincoln 1994; McKay & Marshall 2001). The two-paradigm approach to action research below aims to make action research less marginal for academic readers.

Table 2 — Types of action research and their main characteristics

TYPE OF ACTION RESEARCH	AIMS	FACILITATOR'S ROLE	RELATIONSHIP BETWEEN FACILITATOR AND PARTICIPANTS
1. Technical	effectiveness/efficiency of professional practice professional development	outside 'expert'	co-option (of practitioners who depend on facilitator)
2. Practical	as (1) above practitioner's understanding transformation of their consciousness	Socratic role, encouraging participation and self-reflections	co-operation (process-consultancy)
3. Emancipatory	as (2) above participants' emancipation from the dictates of tradition, self-deception, coercion their critique of bureaucratic systematisation transformation of the organisation and of its system	process moderator (responsibility shared equally by participants)	Collaboration (symmetrical communication)

Note: the numbers in the generalising project refer to the 'standard' chapters of a thesis (this book's Chapter 1), but they could be parts of an article.

Source: Zuber-Skerritt (2001, p. 10), based on Carr and Kemmis (1986).

Core and generalising projects. That is, this chapter argues that an academic researcher should have a core action research project and a generalising action research project. The core project described above and the generalising project of a thesis or an article are not the same (Perry & Zuber-Skerritt 1992, 1994)—'the action research project and your dissertation are not identical' (Coghlan & Brannick 2010, p. 13). The first, core project consists of the normal cycles within a workgroup in one organisation that produces reflection data in the form of journals, memorandums, minutes of meetings and so on.

This spiral of cycles will normally conclude with a report to senior management of that one organisation. In turn, the second, generalising project takes that data from the first project and uses it in its own, normal thesis or article processes of literature review, data collection and analysis, and conclusions that provide analytic generalisation from the findings of the first project (Dick n.d.; Chapter 1). The thesis or article will furnish academic readers with a newly built theory about a phenomenon that exists in several situations. That is, the second, generalising action research project is action research about the first, core action research project. The two projects are linked at the point of data developed during the reflection processes of the first project, as shown in Figure 2. From that point where the researcher switches from the critical theory paradigm to the realism paradigm, the data collection parts of the thesis or article will consist of methodological issues covered in all academic reports such as the steps/spirals taken and their justification, and how issues of validity and reliability were covered through a discussion of research quality described later.

This two-project approach makes the differences between their two underlying paradigms quite explicit. This clear distinction between the paradigm behind each of the two projects makes it easier for the researcher—they do not have to juggle the two paradigms in their head at the same time in a way that is very difficult to do. The aim of the first project is the 'thematic concern' of the workgroup (Kemmis & McTaggart 1988) and the aim of the second project is to fill a gap in the literature that interests readers of academic journals and theses. This two-project structure places equal importance on both paradigms whereas other action research structures place overwhelming emphasis upon the critical theory paradigm (for example, Dick 1999; Herr & Anderson 2005; McNiff & Whitehead 2010), as noted.

Figure 2 — General action research uses two 'projects': core and thesis

```
                    2 ACT              ┌─────────────────────────────┐
                                       │ Core action research project about
                       ↻                │ a group's or individual manager's
                                       │ thematic concern = 'pure' action
                                       │ research
                                       └─────────────────────────────┘
        1 PLAN                3 OBSERVE

                                       ┌─────────────────────────────┐
                                       │ Generalising project about the
                     4 REFLECT         │ thesis' or article's research problem
                                       │ = thesis/article
                                       └─────────────────────────────┘

                  #3 COLLECT DATA

                       ↻

        CH. #1,2 LIT          #4 ANALYSE DATA
        REVIEW


                 #5 CONTRIBUTION TO LITERATURE
```

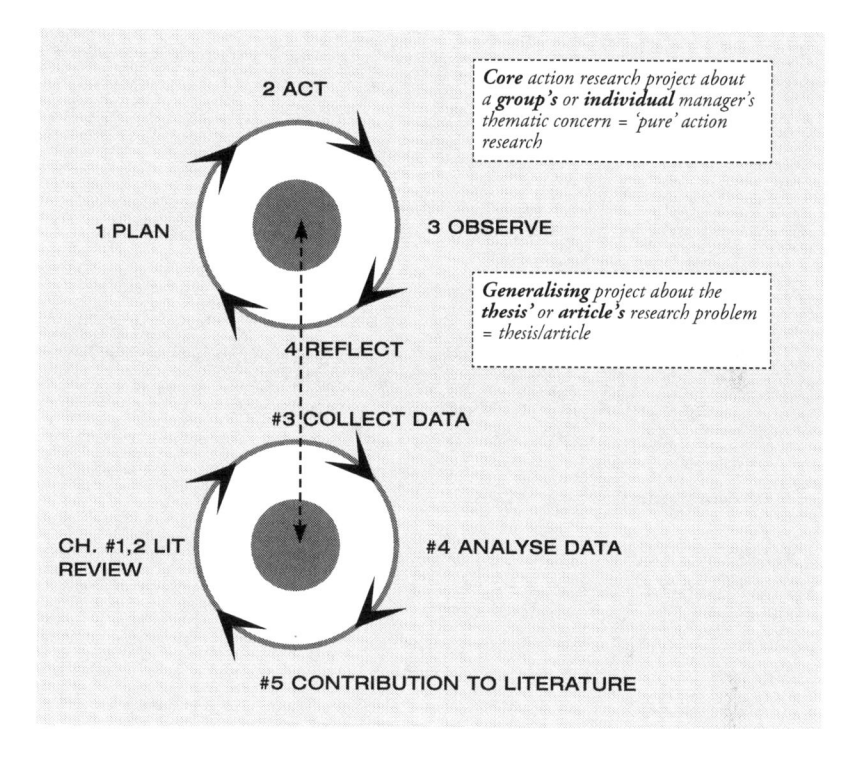

Note: the numbers in the generalising project refer to the 'standard' chapters of a thesis (this book's Chapter 1), but they could be parts of an article.

For example, the core action research report usually requires a detailed story of what took place and self-reflection by the action researcher. But these items are relegated to an appendix in the generalising project's structure or are not even written about at all, because the story and self-reflection occur in *all* academic research and so are not included in a thesis or article at the expense of theory-building issues. That is, readers of a thesis or article know that all academic writing and research is an exercise in the 'progressive reduction of uncertainty' while it is progressively narrowed and refined (Phillips & Pugh 2000, p. 86), and the readers are not interested in those details.

Of course, a thesis or article about the second, generalising stage will have to justify its use of the action research methodology. When could action research be an *appropriate methodology* within an academic research project? There are four justifications for an academic researcher using action research rather than another methodology of data collection (adapting Yin's (2009) justifications for case research in general and for research about a single case in particular):

- Little is known about the research problem—it is a 'pre-paradigmatic' body of knowledge and so an inductive, theory-building methodology is needed.
- Context and phenomenon are not clearly distinct—the research is about a complex social science phenomena that is context-dependent, that is, it investigates the processes in which work people work together.
- The phenomenon is contemporary and dynamic.
- The phenomenon is rarely accessible to academic researchers and the research provides a window on to a critical part of the phenomena.

Examples. Consider an example of how the two core and generalising action research projects can be carried out. Jean had a consulting project to develop a strategic plan for the managers of an innovative architectural practice. She conducted in-depth interviews with the two most senior professionals and then facilitated a strategic planning retreat with all five professionals. These were cycles 1 and 2 of the core action research project. She then developed a five-year plan that incorporated the professionals' visions for change, which was cycle 3. The senior professionals accepted this report and its plan.

It was after that first, core project based on critical theory had finished that she had time to start her second, generalising action research project based on realism. She wrote a thesis about the processes she had used, relating concepts in the literature like Porter's generic strategies and forces of competitive advantage to a professional practice (about which little had been written). As well, she justified why she had done things the ways she had, in particular why she did them differently from the way they were normally done in a large, private firm. Her generalising data was collected from the minutes, reports and journals she had written during the first, core action research project. Not all of this data was relevant to the generalising project's research problem, but much of it was and that part was content analysed for patterns about the generalising research problem. She then said how the findings could be fitted into the literature about strategic planning and used in other types of professional practice and possibly in other organisations, summarised in a new theory that was being built. The first report and thesis were both submitted for her degree.

Consider the structure of an action research thesis or article structure in more detail (based on Perry 1998). An example covers the five thesis 'chapters' of introduction, literature review, methodology, analysis of data, and conclusions and implications:

1. Research problem: How and why can the leadership potential of indigenous staff be developed in large Australian firms?
2. Define 'leadership development' and then review literature about leadership development and indigenous management development, to lead into the core research issues/objectives of the generalising project.
3. Action research methodology: the methodology is justified because the research concerns a complex social situation about which little is known, as noted above; the thematic concern is how we as senior managers can develop indigenous staff in my firm, using three plan-act-observe-reflect cycles described in detail; the paradigmatic issues are discussed, as is validity and reliability, and ethical issues.
4. Analyse the reflection data from the 3 cycles of the core action research project
5. Analytical generalisation of the analysed data to other organisations in Australia and overseas, so that a new theory about the research problem is built.

In brief, it is possible to write a report of an action research project done within the critical theory paradigm that will interest readers of journal articles and theses who operate within the realism paradigm. Each paradigm has its own, self-evident worldview, but they can be bridged where reflection data feeds into the academic report.

CRITERIA FOR JUDGING THE QUALITY OF ACTION RESEARCH PROJECTS

Because there are two worldviews in the research project, there are two ways of assessing the quality of a complete action research project (this discussion closely follows Thompson & Perry 2004). Because a paradigm is a worldview, the quality of scientific research can only be judged in terms specific to the paradigm under which the researcher is working (Healy & Perry 2000), that is, the criteria in one paradigm could be almost meaningless in another. Thus the findings of one project cannot be transferred to a project in another paradigm without changing their form and content. This section discusses the several criteria that can be applied to establish research rigor within the core action research 'project', and to the generalising research 'project'. It demonstrates that different sets of criteria are needed for each of the critical theory and realism paradigms that appear to underlie the two projects.

Consider those two sets of criteria. The criteria within the *critical theory* paradigm used to judge the value of the core action research project can be assumed to be those of all subjective research: truth value/credibility, applicability/ transferability, consistency/dependability, neutrality/confirmability (Lincoln & Guba 1985). In each of these four pairs, the latter term is an operationalisation of the former. In turn, the criteria in the *realism* paradigm used to judge the quality of the generalising research project are: ontological appropriateness, contingent validity, multiple perceptions about a single reality, methodological trustworthiness, analytic generalisation and construct validity (Healy & Perry 1998).

Tables 3 and 4 show these two sets of quality criteria were addressed in a doctoral thesis that used the action research methodology (Thompson 2003, pp. 106-111).

CONCLUSION

In summary, scientific paradigms are coherent worldviews that are appropriate for different phenomena. Of these paradigms, the critical theory paradigm underlies action research and the realism paradigm underlies most academic social science research. Blending those two paradigms in two separate projects—a core action research project and a generalising action research project—is one way of handling the gulf between them, with a link between them at the reflection point of the core action research project. The result is an adjustment to a body of knowledge about a social science phenomenon that is an improvement on the sketchy picture in the literature that existed when the research began. Criteria to judge each of the two projects can be established. In conclusion, action research and social science can be combined.

Table 3 — Criteria used to demonstrate rigour of the core action research within the critical theory paradigm

		CRITICAL THEORY		
No.	Criterion (operationalised criterion in bold) (a)	Aim of criterion and measures applied to achieve criterion (b)	Phase of research techniques were used (c)	Measures applied within this research (d)
1	Truth value/	Demonstrate that multiple constructions have been represented adequately and that they are credible to the constructors of the original multiple realities	Data collection and analysis	Use of data from multiple sources. Identification, determination and analysis of patterns in the research data
	Credibility	Carry out inquiry in a manner that increases probability that the findings will be found to be credible and demonstrate the credibility of findings by having them approved by constructors	Sections: 3.2, 3.5, 3.10, Chapter 4	Data triangulation. Offer of research findings to respondents for review. Review and affirmation of research findings by those respondents

Table 3 — Criteria used to demonstrate rigour of the core action research within the critical theory paradigm (contd)

		CRITICAL THEORY		
No.	Criterion (operationalised criterion in bold) (a)	Aim of criterion and measures applied to achieve criterion (b)	Phase of research techniques were used (c)	Measures applied within this research (d)
2	Applicability	Acknowledging that only working hypotheses may be abstracted from a study, the research provides sufficient descriptive data to allow future investigations into similar circumstances	Research design Data collection and analysis	Action research approach Interview protocol of semi-structured interview Integration of research problem and research issues with Chapter 5 of this research Provision of a Database
	Transferability	Provide a thick description of the study in the Database that allows transferability judgements with regards to context for possible future empirical testing (Lincoln & Guba 1985, p. 316)	Post data analysis Sections: 3.2, 3.4, Database	

Table 3 — Criteria used to demonstrate rigour of the core action research within the critical theory paradigm (contd)

	CRITICAL THEORY			
No.	Criterion (operationalised criterion in bold) (a)	Aim of criterion and measures applied to achieve criterion (b)	Phase of research techniques were used (c)	Measures applied within this research (d)
3	Consistency **Dependability**	Means for taking into account factors of instability and factors of phenomenal or design induced change Inquiry audit to determine fairness of the process of the inquiry	Research design Sections 3.2, 3.4, 3.8, 3.7, Database	Action research process Interview protocol of semi-structured interviews Detailed description of how data was collected Review by supervisors PhD research in progress workshop delivery Compilation of research documents Development of research Database/audit trail described in section 3.2

Table 3 — Criteria used to demonstrate rigour of the core action research within the critical theory paradigm (contd)

CRITICAL THEORY				
No.	Criterion (operationalised criterion in bold) (a)	Aim of criterion and measures applied to achieve criterion (b)	Phase of research techniques were used (c)	Measures applied within this research (d)
4	Neutrality **Confirmability**	Demonstrate that data is reliable, factual, confirmable or confirmed An audit trail has been developed so that accuracy of research and data can be established. This includes the ability of interested parties to examine data, findings, interpretations and recommendations	Data collection and analysis Sections: 3.2 Database 3	Documentation of agreements with sponsor enterprise Documentation of implementation of action research methodology Interview protocols and tapes and transcriptions of interviews Development of research Database/ audit trail described in section 3.2 including; internal memos, notes from discussions, bid documentation, draft documents

Source: synthesised from Aaker & Day (1990); Azhar (2001); Burns (1994); Carson et al. (2001); Gummeson (1998); Healy & Perry (2000); Hirshman (1986); Lincoln & Guba (1985); Master (1999); O'Leary (2000); Parkhe (1993); Yin (1994); Zikmund (1997).

Table 4 — Criteria used to demonstrate rigour of the generalising research project within the realism paradigm

		REALISM		
No.	Criterion (a)	Aim of criterion and measures applied to achieve criterion (b)	Phase of research techniques were used (c)	Measures applied within this research (d)
1	**Ontology** Ontological appropriateness	The research problem deals with complex social science phenomena involving reflective people Demonstrating that the world being investigated is 'world three'—that is the independent creations of minds or living creatures or the 'world of ideas, art, science, language, ethics, institutions ...' (Popper in Magee 1985, p. 61)	Research design and analysis, Sections: Chapter 1, Chapter 2, 3.2, 3.4, 3.8, 3.7, Chapter 4, Chapter 5, Database	Formulation of research question Use of prior theory Literature review Action research design Semi-structured interviewing Triangulation of data Development of research Database/audit trail described in section 3.2
2	Contingent validity	Establishes validity about generative mechanisms that are named and discovered by the research and the contexts that make them contingent	Research design and analysis, Sections: 3.4, 3.8, 3.8.1, Database	Action research design Semi-structured interviewing Details of organisational circumstances and action research context Development of research Database/ audit trail described in section3.2

Table 4 — Criteria used to demonstrate rigour of the generalising research project within the realism paradigm (contd)

		REALISM		
No.	Criterion (a)	Aim of criterion and measures applied to achieve criterion (b)	Phase of research techniques were used (c)	Measures applied within this research (d)
3	**Epistemology** Multiple perceptions of participants and of peer researchers	Demonstrate how the research reveals the real world, albeit in a manner that is only imperfectly and probabilistically comprehensible. Focus not on value-free or value-laden but value awareness of the research	Research design and analysis, Sections: 3.10.2, 3.2, 3.7, Chapter 4, Chapter 5	Multiple data sources Presentation of supporting evidence in Table 3.1 Broad questioning in interviewing before probe questions Triangulation of data Awareness of own values and their impact on data collection Supervisor and peer review
4	**Methodology** Methodological trustworthiness	Establish audibility of the report	Research design and analysis, Sections: Database, Appendix 6, Appendix 9, Chapter 4	Development of research Database/audit trail described in section 2.2 Use of frequent and relevant quotations in report to support theory building Descriptions of procedures with details of dates, respondents and time

Table 4 — Criteria used to demonstrate rigour of the generalising research project within the realism paradigm (contd)

		REALISM		
No.	Criterion (a)	Aim of criterion and measures applied to achieve criterion (b)	Phase of research techniques were used (c)	Measures applied within this research (d)
5	**Analytic generalisation**	Establish the primacy of theory-building in the report	Research design and analysis, Sections: 2.5.3, 3.3, Chapter 4, Chapter 5	Identification of research issues before data collection. Development of theory through triangulation of data. No use of quantitative techniques

Table 4 — Criteria used to demonstrate rigour of the generalising research project within the realism paradigm (contd)

	REALISM			
No.	Criterion (a)	Aim of criterion and measures applied to achieve criterion (b)	Phase of research techniques were used (c)	Measures applied within this research (d)
6	**Construct validity**	Determine how well constructs in the theory being built are measured by the research	Data collection Sections: Chapter 2, 3.7, Table 3.1, Chapter 3, Database, Chapter 2, Section	Literature review Semi-structured interviews Interviews with experts in different fields Development and use of protocols for interviews Interviews with project partner management and staff Core action research Examination of funding agency publications Examination of tender documents Data referencing Development of Database Table 2.1 detailing chain of evidence as described in Database Copies of transcripts were provided to informants for confirmation and comment Review of draft versions by supervisor/ peers

Source: synthesised from Aaker & Day (1990); Azhar (2001); Burns (1994); Carson et al. (2001); Gummeson (1998); Healy & Perry (2000); Hirschman

(1986); Lincoln & Guba (1985); Master (1999); O'Leary (2000); Parkhe (1993); Yin (1994); Zikmund (1997).

ACKNOWLEDGEMENTS

This chapter is closely based on and even incorporates some parts of reports by Thompson and Perry (2004), Perry (2000), Perry and Rao (2007), Zuber-Skerrit and Perry (2002), and Perry and Sankaran (2002). The discussion of paradigms is based on Perry (2000), Perry, Riege and Brown (1999), and Sobh and Perry (2006). I deeply thank all my co-authors.

REFERENCES

Abraham, S 2012, *Work-applied Learning for Change*, AIB, Adelaide (available from amazon.com and bookdepository.com).

Adams, GB & White, JD 1994, 'Dissertation research in public administration and cognate fields: an assessment of methods and quality', *Public Administration Review*, vol. 54, no. 6, pp. 565–576.

Alrichter, H, Kemmis, S, McTaggart, R & Zuber-Skerrit, O 2000, 'The concept of action research', in *Action Learning, Action Research and Process Management: Theory, Practice, Praxis*, ed. Action Research Unit, Faculty of Education, Griffith University, Brisbane.

Armstrong, JS 1982, 'Research in scientific journals: implications for editors and authors', *Journal of Forecasting*, vol. 1, pp. 83–104.

Armstrong, JS 1985, *Long Range Forecasting: from Crystal Ball to Computer*, Wiley Interscience, New York.

Armstrong JS 1997, 'Peer review for journals: evidence on quality control, fairness, and innovation', *Science and Engineering Ethics*, vol. 3, pp. 63–84.

Armstrong, JS & Overton, TS 1977, 'Estimating nonresponse bias in mail surveys', *Journal of Marketing Research*, vol. 14, pp. 396–402.

Basari, A Halim Bin Haji 2009, 'Managing healthcare supply chains in an armed forces environment', PhD thesis, Australian Institute of Business, Adelaide.

'Basics of APA Style Manual' 2012, Australian Psychological Association, viewed 29 July 2012, <http://flash1r.apa.org/apastyle/basics/>.

Bauer, MW & Gaskell, G 2000, *Qualitative Researching with Text, Image and Sound: a Practical Handbook*, Sage, London, pp. 38–56.

Belcher, WL 2009a, *Writing Your Journal Article in Twelve Weeks: a Guide to Academic Publishing Success*, Sage, Thousand Oaks.

Belcher, WL 2009b, 'Responding to a journal's decision to reject', *IETE Technical Review*, vol. 26, no. 6, pp. 391–393.

Bem DJ 2002, 'Writing the empirical journal article', Cornell University, viewed 14 August 2011, <http://dbem.ws/WritingArticle.pdf>.

Bertaux, D 1981, 'From the life-history approach to the transformation of sociological practice', in *Biography and Society: the Life History Approach in the Social Science*, ed. D Bertaux, Sage, London, pp. 29–45.

Bloom, BS & Krathowl, DR 1956, *Taxonomy of Educational Objectives*, McKay & Co., New York.

Boal, LB & Trank, CQ 2011, '*Journal of Management Inquiry* at 20: Still crazy after all these years', *Journal of Management Inquiry*, vol. 20, no. 4, pp. 343–348.

Bogle, JC 2009, *Enough: True Measures of Money, Business and Life*, Wiley, Hoboken, New Jersey.

Brown, R 1995, 'The "big picture" about managing the writing process', in *Quality in Postgraduate Education—Issues and Processes*, ed. O Zuber-Skerritt, Kogan Page, Sydney, pp. 90–109.

Brown, RF, Rogers, DJ & Pressland, AJ 1994, 'Create a clear focus: the "big picture" about writing better research articles', *American Entomologist*, vol. 40, no. 3, pp. 144–145.

Brown, R 1996, *Key Skills for Publishing Research Articles*, Write Way Consulting, Brisbane.

Calder, BJ 1980, 'Focus group interview and qualitative research in organisations', in Organisational Assessment, eds EE Lawler, DA Nadler & C Cammann, C, John Wiley and Sons New York.

Carr, W & Kemmis, S 1986, *Becoming Critical: Education, Knowledge and Action Research*, Deakin University Press, Geelong, Victoria.

Carson, D, Gilmore, A, Gronhaug, K & Perry, C 2001, *Qualitative Research in Marketing*, Sage, London.

Carson, D, Gilmore, A, & Perry C 2006, 'Academic publishing: best practice for editors, authors and reviewers', *European Business Review*, special issue on academic publishing and academic journals, vol.18, no. 6, pp. 468–478.

Charmaz, K 2006, *Constructing Grounded Theory: a Practical Guide Through Qualitative Analysis*, Sage, Thousand Oaks.

Chetty, S & Stangl, L 2010, 'Internationalization and innovation in a network relationship context', *European Journal of Marketing*, vol. 44, no. 11/12, pp. 1724–1743.

Clark, D & Gibbs, GR 2008, *Prof. Nigel King on template analysis: section 3 comparison with other coding approaches*, viewed 7 November 2011, <http://onlineqda.hud.ac.uk/_REQUALLO/FR/Template_Analysis/Index.php>.

Clark, N 1986, 'Writing-up the doctoral thesis', *Graduate Management Research*, Autumn, pp. 25–31.

Coghlan, D & Brannick, T 2010, *Doing Action Research in Your Own Organisation*, 3rd edn, Sage, London.

Conrad, L, Perry, C & Zuber-Skerritt, O 1992, 'Alternatives to traditional postgraduate supervision in the social sciences', in Zuber-Skerritt, O. (ed), *Starting Research—Supervision and Training*, Tertiary Education Institute, University of Queensland, Brisbane, pp. 137–151.

Coolican, H 1990, *Research Methods and Statistics in Psychology*, Hodder and Stoughton, London.

Cooper, HM 1989, *Integrating Research a Guide for Literature Reviews*, Sage, Newbury Park.

Crawford, M & Di Benetto, A 2008, *New Products Management*, 9th edn, McGraw Hill, New York.

Day, A n.d., 'How to write publishable papers', viewed 20 October 2012, <http://sigma.poligran.edu.co/politecnico/apoyo/Decisiones/curso/howtowriteclean.pdf>.

Day, A 1996, *How To Get Research Published in Journals*, 1st edn, Gower, Aldershot.

Day, A 2007, *How To Get Research Published in Journals*, 2nd edn, Gower, Aldershot.

de Ruyter, K & Scholl, N 1998, 'Positioning qualitative research: reflections from theory and practice', *Qualitative Market Research: an International Journal*, vol. 1, no. 1, pp. 7–14.

Derricourt, R 1992, 'Diligent thesis to high-flying book: an unlikely metamorphosis', *Australian Campus Review Weekly*, 27 February–4 March, p. 13.

Dick, B n.d., 'You want to do an action research thesis?', viewed 26 November 2012, <http://www.aral.com.au/resources/arthesis.html#a_art_writing>.

Dick, B 1997, 'Approaching an action research thesis', viewed 27 November 2012, http://www.aral.com.au/resources/phd.html.

Dick, B 1990, *Convergent Interviewing*, Interchange, Brisbane.

Dubois, A & Araujo, L 2004, 'Research methods in industrial marketing studies', in *Rethinking Marketing: Developing a New Understanding of Markets*, eds H. Håkansson, D.Harrison, & A. Waluszewski, Wiley, Chichester, pp. 207–227.

Easterby-Smith, M, Golden-Biddle, K & Locke K 2008, 'Working with pluralism: determining quality in qualitative research', *Organizational Research Methods*, vol. 11, no. 3, pp. 419–429.

Easterby-Smith, M, Thorpe, R & Lowe, A 1991, *Management Research: an Introduction*, Sage, London.

Easterby-Smith, M, Thorpe, R & Lowe, A 2008, *Management Research: an Introduction*, 3rd edn, Sage, London.

Ehrenreich, B 2001, *Nickel and Dimed*, Owl, New York.

Eisenhardt, K 1989, 'Building theory from case study research', *Academy of Management Review*, vol. 14, no. 4, pp. 532–50.

Eisenhardt, KM & Graebner, ME 2007, 'Theory building from cases: opportunities and challenges', *Academy of Management Journal*, vol. 50, no.1, pp. 25–32.

Eisenhardt, KM & Zbaracki, M J 1992, 'Strategic decision making', *Strategic Management Journal*, vol. 13, pp. 17–37.

Emory, CW & Cooper, DR 1991, *Business Research Methods*, Irwin, Homewood.

Faigley, L 2012, *The Little Penguin Handbook: Australasian Edition*, Penguin, Sydney.

Fiske, DW & Fogg, L 1990, 'But the reviewers are making different criticisms of my paper! Diversity and uniqueness in reviewers' comments', *American Psychologist*, vol. 45, no. 5, pp. 591–598.

Flyvberg, B 2006, 'Five misunderstandings about case-study research', *Qualitative Inquiry*, vol. 12, no. 1, pp. 219–245.

Frost, P & Stablein, R 1992, *Doing Exemplary Research*, Sage, Newbury Park.

Gable, GG 1994, 'Integrating case study and survey research methods: an example in information systems', *European Journal of Information Systems*, vol. 3, no. 2, pp. 112–126.

Gaskell, G 2000, 'Individual and group interviewing', in *Qualitative Research in Text, Image and Sound*, eds M Bauer & G Gaskell, G, Sage, London, pp. 38–56.

Gibbs, GR & Taylor, C 2010, *How and what to code,* viewed 1 December 2012, <http://onlineqda.hud.ac.uk/Intro_QDA/how_what_to_code.php>.

Gibbert, M & Ruigrok, W 2010, 'The "what" and "how" of case study rigor: three strategies based on published work', *Organizational Research Methods*, vol. 13, no. 4, pp. 710–737.

Gilmore, A, Carson, D & Perry, C 2006, 'Academic publishing: best practice for editors, guest editors, authors and reviewers', *European Business Review*, special issue on academic publishing and academic journals, vol. 18, no.6, pp. 468–478.

Glanville, Samsukri Glanville bin Mohamad 2009, 'How professional security investors in Malaysia process their investment decisions', PhD thesis, Australian Institute of Business, Adelaide.

Gordon, W & Langmaid, R 1988, *Qualitative Marketing Research*, Gower, Aldershot.

Greene, JC & Caracelli, VJ 2002, 'Making paradigmatic sense of mixed methods practice', in *Handbook of Mixed Methods in Social & Behavioral Research*, eds T Tashakkori & C Teddlie, Sage, Thousand Oaks, pp. 91–110.

Green, J & Thorogood, N 2009, *Qualitative Methods for Health Research*, 2nd edn, Sage, Thousand Oaks.

Gross, MA & Pullman, M 2012, 'Playing their roles: experiential design concepts applied in complex services', *Journal of Management Inquiry*, vol. 21, no. 1, pp. 43–59.

Guba, EG & Lincoln, YS 1994, 'Competing paradigms in qualitative research', in *Handbook of Qualitative Research*, eds NK Denzin & YS Lincoln, Sage, Thousand Oaks.

Guba, EG & Lincoln, YS 2005, 'Paradigmatic controversies, contradictions, and emerging confluence', in *The Sage Handbook of Qualitative Research*, eds NK Denzin & Y S Lincoln, Sage, Thousand Oaks, pp. 105–117.

Guest, G, Bunce, A & Johnson, L 2006, 'How many interviews are enough? An experiment with data saturation and variability', *Field Methods*, vol. 18, no. 1, pp. 59–82.

Gummesson, E 2000, *Qualitative Methods in Management Research*, Sage, London.

Hacker, D 2009, *Rules for Writers with 2009 MLA and 2010 APA Updates*, Bedford/St Martins, Boston.

Hair, JF, Anderson, RE, Tatham, RL & Black, WC 1995, *Multivariate Data Analysis with Readings*, Prentice Hall, Englewood Cliffs.

Hanson, D & Grimmer, M 2007, 'The mix of qualitative and quantitative research in major marketing journals 1993-2002', *European Journal of Marketing*, vol. 41, no. 1/2, pp. 58–70.

Harzing, AW 2007, 'Publish or Perish', viewed 21 December 2011, <http://www.harzing.com/pop.htm>.

Hassard, J 1990, 'Multiple paradigms and organisational analysis: a case study', *Organisational Studies*, vol. 12, iss. 2, pp. 275–299.

Healy, M and Perry, C 2000, 'Comprehensive criteria to judge the validity and reliability of qualitative research within the realism paradigm', *Qualitative Market Research—an International Journal*, volume 3, number 3, pp. 118–126.

Heide, JB 1994, 'Interorganisational governance in marketing channels', *Journal of Marketing*, vol. 58, pp. 71–85.

Herr, K & Anderson, GL 2005, *The Action Research Dissertation: a Guide for Students and Faculty*, Sage, London.

Hollway, W & Jefferson, T 2000, *Doing Qualitative Research Differently, Free Association, Narrative And The Interview Method*, Sage, London.

Hubbard, R & Armstrong, JS 1994, 'Replications and extensions in marketing: rarely published but quite contrary', *International Journal of Research in Marketing*, vol. 11, pp. 233–248.

Hubbard, R & Vetter, DE 1996., 'An empirical comparison of published replications research in economics, finance, management and marketing', *Journal of Business Research*, vol. 35, pp. 153–164.

Huff, AS 1999, *Writing for Scholarly Publication*, Sage, Thousand Oaks.

Hunt, S 1991, *Modern Marketing Theory*, South-Western, Cincinnati.

Jonnson, S 2006, 'On academic writing', *European Business Review*, vol. 18, no. 6, pp. 479–490.

Kallestinova, ED 2011, 'How to write your first research paper', *Yale Journal of Biology and Medicine*, vol. 84, no. 3, pp. 181–190.

Kasper, H, Lehrer, M, Muhlbacher, J & Muller, B 2010, 'Thinking knowledge: an interpretive field study of knowledge-sharing practices of firms in three multinational contexts', *Journal of Management Inquiry*, vol. 19, no. 4, pp. 367–381.

Kemmis, S & McTaggart, R 1988, *The Action Research Planner*, 3rd edition, Deakin University Press, Australia.

King, N & Horrocks, C 2010, *Interviews in Qualitative Research*, Sage, Los Angeles.

Kohli, A 1989, 'Determinants of influence in organisational buying: a contingency approach', *Journal of Marketing*, vol. 53, July, pp. 319–332.

Krathwohl, DR 1977, *How to Prepare a Research Proposal*, University of Syracuse, Syracuse.

Kvale, S 1996, *Interviews: an Introduction to Qualitative Research Interviewing*, Sage, Thousand Oaks.

Leedy, P 1989, *Practical Research*, Macmillan, New York.

Lincoln, Y & Guba, E 1985, *Naturalistic Inquiry*, Sage, Newbury Park.

Lincoln, YS & Guba, G 1986, *Naturalistic Inquiry*, Sage, London.

Lindsay, D 1995, *A Guide to Scientific Writing*, Longman, Melbourne.

Loh, E 2011, 'Medical doctors and hospital management', PhD thesis, Australian Institute of Business (available from ninaeau@yahoo.com).

Madsen, TK 1989, 'Successful exporting management: some empirical evidence', *International Marketing Review*, vol. 6, no. 4, pp. 41–57.

Magee, B 1985, *Popper*, 3rd edn, Fontana, London.

Marshall, C & Rossman, GB 1995, *Designing Qualitative Research*, 2nd edn, Sage, Newbury Park.

Massingham, KR 1984, 'Pitfalls along the thesis approach to a higher degree', *The Australian*, 25 July, p. 15, quoted in Nightingale, P, 'Examination of research theses', *Higher Education Research and Development*, vol. 3, no. 2, pp. 137–150.

Mason, M 2010, 'Sample size and saturation in PhD studies using qualitative interviews', *Forum Qualitative Science Research*, vol. 11, no. 3, p. 8 (available at http://www.qualitative-research.net/index.php/fqs/article/viewArticle/1428/3027).

Master, H & Prideaux, B 1998, 'Culture and vacation satisfaction: a study of Taiwanese tourists in South East Queensland', *Tourism Management*, vol. 21, no. 5, pp. 445–449.

Matchett, S 2010, 'Ivory tower myopia ails marketing', *The Australian*, 17 March, p. 30.

Maykut, P & Morehouse, R 1994, *Beginning Qualitative Research: a Philosophical and Practical Guide*, Burgess Science Press.

McGilchrist, I 2009, *The Master and His Emissary: the Divided Brain and the Reshaping Of Western Civilisation*, viewed 25 February 2012, <http://www.abc.net.au/radionational/programs/allinthemind/the-master-and-his-emissary-the-divided-brain-and/2959006>.

McKay, J & Marshall, P 2001, 'The dual imperatives of action research', *Information Technology* and People, vol. 14, no. 1, pp. 45–59.

McKinsey 1994, *The Wealth of Ideas*, Australian Manufacturing Council, Melbourne.

McNiff, J & Whitehead, J 2010, *You and Your Action Research Project*, 3rd edn, Routledge, Abingdon.

Miles, MB & Huberman, AM 1994a, *Qualitative Data Analysis*, Sage, New York.

Miles, MB & Huberman, AM 1994b, *An Expanded Sourcebook: Qualitative Data Analysis*, Sage, Thousand Oaks.

Morelli, J 2010, 'Strategic marketing in the Australian funeral industry', DBA thesis, Gibaran Graduate School of Business, Adelaide.

Morgan, DL & Krueger, RA 1993, 'When to use focus groups and why', in *Successful Focus Groups*, ed. DL Morgan, Sage, London.

Morgan, DL 1993, *Successful Focus Groups: Advance The State Of Art*, Sage, Thousand Oaks.

Morse, JM 2000, 'Determining sample size' *Qualitative Health Research*, vol. 19, no. 3, pp. 3–5.

Moses, I 1985, *Supervising Postgraduates*, HERDSA, Sydney.

Mullins, G and Kiley, M 2002, '"It's a PhD, not a Nobel Prize": how experienced examiners assess research theses', *Studies in Higher Education*, vol. 27, no. 4, pp. 369–386.

Murray, R 2002, *How to Write a Thesis*, 2nd edn, Open University Press, Maidenhead.

Murray, R 2009, *Writing for Academic Journals*, 2nd edn, McGraw-Hill Education, London.

Nair, GS & Riege, AM 1995, 'Using convergent interviewing to develop the research problem of a postgraduate thesis', Proceedings of Marketing Education and Researchers International Conference, Gold Coast.

Neuman, WL 2000, *Social Research Methods: Qualitative and Quantitative Approaches*, 4th edn, Allyn and Bacon: Boston.

Neuman, WL 2007, *Basics of Social Research: Qualitative and Quantitative Approaches*, Allyn and Bacon, Boston.

Nightingale, P 1984, 'Examination of research theses', *Higher Education Research and Development*, vol. 3, no. 2, pp. 137–152.

Nightingale, P 1992, 'Initiation into research through writing', in Zuber-Skerritt, O (ed) 1992, *Starting Research - Supervision and Training*, Tertiary Education Institute, University of Queensland, Brisbane.

Nuance Communications 2012, 'Transcribing interviews', viewed 12 December 2012, <http://australia.nuance.com/for-individuals/by-industry/education-solutions/transcribing-interview/index.htm>.

O'Brien, JP, Drnevich, P, Crook, TR & Armstrong, CE 2010, 'Does business school research add economic value for students?', *Academy of Management Learning & Education*, vol. 9, no. 4, pp. 638–651.

Ozcan, P & Eisenhardt, KM 2009, 'Origin of alliance portfolios: entrepreneurs, network strategies, and firm performance', *Academy of Management Journal*, vol. 52, no. 2, pp. 246–279.

Palmer, D, Dick, B & Freiburger, N 2009, 'Rigor and relevance in organization studies', *Journal of Management Inquiry*, vol. 18, no. 4, pp. 265–272.

Pannell, DJ 2002, 'Prose, psychopaths and persistence: personal perspectives on publishing', *Canadian Journal of Agricultural Economics*, vol. 50, iss. 2, pp. 115.

Parkhe, A 1993, '"Messy" research, methodological predispositions, and theory development in international joint ventures', *Academy of Management Review*, vol. 18, no. 2, pp. 227–268.

Patton, MQ 2002, *Qualitative Evaluation and Research Methods*, 3rd edn, Sage, Newbury Park.

Pawson, R & Tilley, N 1997, *Realistic Evaluation*, Sage, London.

Perry, C 1997, 'How can I write a journal article in two days?' A book review of Day, A. 1997, "How to get research published in journals", *European Journal of Marketing*, vol. 31, no. 11/12, pp. 896–901.

Perry, C 1998a & 2012, 'A structured approach for presenting theses', *Australasian Marketing Journal*, vol. 6, no.1, pp. 63–85 (An updated 2012 version is at http://search.scu.edu.au/?q=perry&c=0%2C1%2C2).

Perry, C 1998b, 'Processes of a case study methodology for postgraduate research in marketing', *European Journal of Marketing*, vol. 32, issue 9/10, pp. 785–802.

Perry, C 2000, 'Realism also rules OK: scientific paradigms and case research in marketing', in *Applying Qualitative Methods to Marketing Management Research*, eds R Buber, J Gadner & L Richards, Palgrave Macmillan, Houndmills (UK), pp. 46–60.

Perry, C 2001, 'Case research in marketing', *The Marketing Review*, vol. 1 no. 1, pp. 303–323.

Perry, C 2004, 'Realism also rules OK: Scientific paradigms and case research in marketing' in *Applying Qualitative Methods To Marketing Management Research*, eds R Buber, J Gadber & L Richards, Palgrave Macmillan, New York, pp. 46–60.

Perry C 2011, 'A structured approach to the journey of doctoral research', *International Journal of Organisational Behaviour*, vol. 16, no. 1, pp. 1–12, viewed 28 October 2012, <http://www.usq.edu.au/business-law/research/ijob/articles>.

Perry, C, Carson, D & Gilmore, A 2003, 'Joining a conversation: writing for EJM's editors, reviewers and readers requires planning, care and persistence', *European Journal of Marketing*, vol. 37, iss. 6/7, 652–667.

Perry, C & Rao, S 2007, 'Action research in enterprise research', in *Innovative Methodologies in Enterprise Research*, eds D Hine D & D Carson D, Edward Elgar, Northampton, Massachusetts, pp. 124–136.

Perry, C, Reige, A & Brown, L 1998, 'Realism rules OK: scientific paradigms in marketing research about networks', Australia and New Zealand Marketing Academy Conference (ANZMAC98), University of Otago, Dunedin, New Zealand, December.

Perry, C, Reige, A & Brown, L 1999, 'Realism's role among scientific paradigms in marketing research', *Irish Marketing Review*, vol. 12, no. 2, pp. 16–23.

Perry, C & Sankaran, S 2002, 'Practical methods in collecting and analyzing information while conducting action research in organisations for academic research', distributed paper, XVth World Congress of Sociology in Brisbane, Australia, July 7–13.

Perry, C & Zuber-Skerritt, O 1992, 'Action research in graduate management research programs', *Higher Education*, vol. 23, March, pp. 195–208.

Perry, C & Zuber-Skerritt, O 1994, 'Doctorates by action research for senior practicing managers', *Management Learning*, vol. 1, no. 1, March, pp. 341–364.

Peters, DP & Ceci, SJ 1982, 'Peer review practices of psychological journals: the fate of published articles, submitted again, and its open peer commentary', *The Behavioural and Brain Sciences*, vol. 5, pp. 187–255.

Peters, P 1995, *The Cambridge Australian English Style Guide*, Cambridge University Press, Cambridge.

Pettigrew, S 1999, 'Culture and consumption a study of beer consumption in Australia', PhD thesis, University of Western Australia.

Phillips, EM & Conrad, L 1992, 'Creating a supportive environment for postgraduate study', in *Manual for conducting Workshops on Postgraduate Supervision*, ed. O Zuber-Skerritt, Tertiary Education Institute, University of Queensland, Brisbane, pp. 153–163.

Phillips, EM 1992, 'The PhD—assessing quality at different stages of its development', in *Starting Research—Supervision and Training*, ed. O Zuber-Skerritt, Tertiary Education Institute, University of Queensland, Brisbane.

Phillips, EM & Pugh, DS 2000, *How to Get a PhD*, 3rd edn, Open University Press, Milton Keynes.

Piekkari, R, Welch, C & Paavilainen, E 2009 'The case study as disciplinary convention : evidence from international business journals', *Organizational Research Methods*, vol. 12, no. 3, pp. 567–589.

Poole, ME 1993, 'Reviewing for research excellence: expectations, procedures and outcomes', *Australian Journal of Education*, vol. 37, no. 3, pp. 219–230.

Rao, S 2002, 'The impact of Internet use on inter-firm relationships in service industries', PhD thesis, Griffith University, Brisbane.

Rao, S & Perry, C 2003, 'Convergent interviewing to build a theory in under-researched areas: Principles and an example investigation of Internet usage in inter-firm relationship', *Qualitative Market Research*, vol. 6, no. 4, pp. 236–47.

Rao, S 2004, 'The Internet and business-to-business relational bonds: perspectives from an Australian service industry', *International Journal of Internet and Advertising*, vol. 1, no. 4, pp. 12–29.

Rao, S and Perry, C 2007, 'Convergent interviewing: a starting methodology for an enterprise research program', in *Innovative Methodologies in Enterprise Research*, eds D Hine & D Carson, Edward Elgar, Northampton, Massachusetts, pp. 86–100.

Reason, P & Bradbury, H 2008, *The SAGE Handbook of Action Research: Participative Inquiry and Practice*, 2nd edn, Sage, London.

Riege, AM 2003, 'Validity and reliability tests in case study research: a literature review with 'hands-on' applications for each research phase', *Qualitative Market Research: An International Journal*, vol. 6, no. 2, pp. 75–86.

Rocco, TS & Hatcher 2011, *The Handbook of Scholarly Writing and Publishing*, Jossey-Bass, San Francisco.

Rocco TS & Plathotnik M 2011, 'Increasing the odds of publishing a qualitative manuscript', in *The Handbook of Scholarly Writing and Publishing*, eds TS Rocco & T Hatcher, Jossey-Bass , San Francisco, pp. 161–178.

Rogers, EM 1983, *Diffusion of Innovation*, The Free Press, New York.

Saunders, J & Hirst, A 2000, 'And you thought it was bad: the editorial process of journals', AM2000 Proceedings, Academy of Marketing Conference, 5–7 July, University of Derby, Nottingham.

Sekaran, U 2000, *Research Methods for Business: a Skill Building Approach*, John Wiley and Sons.

Silverman 2008, 'Qualitative Methods', National Institutes of Health, viewed 29 October 2012, <http://www.esourceresearch.org/eSourceBook/QualitativeMethods/13References/tabid/279/Default.aspx>.

Skapinker, M 2008, 'Why business ignores the business schools', *Financial Times*, 7 January.

Smith, R 2006, 'Peer review: a flawed process at the heart of science and journals', *Journal of the Royal Society of Medicine*, vol. 99, no. 4, pp. 178–82.

Sobh, R & Perry, C 2006, 'Research design and data analysis in realism research', *European Journal of Marketing*, vol. 40, no. 11/12, pp. 1194–1209.

Stake, R 2005, 'Qualitative case studies', in *The Sage Handbook of Qualitative Research*, 3rd edn, eds NK Denzin & YS Lincoln, Sage, Thousand Oaks, pp. 433–466.

Stewart, DW 2002, 'Getting published: reflections of an old editor', *Journal of Marketing*, October, vol. 66, iss. 4, pp. 1–6.

Stokes, R 2004, 'Inter-organisational relationships for events tourism strategy making in Australian states and territories', PhD thesis, Griffith University, Brisbane (available from www.scholar.google.com).

Stokes, R and Perry, C 2007, 'Case research about enterprises', in *Innovative Methodologies in Enterprise Research*, eds D Hine D and D Carson D, Edward Elgar, Northampton, Massachusetts.

Style Manual for Authors, Editors and Printers 2002, 6th edn, Wiley, Brisbane.

Summers, JO 2002, 'Guidelines for conducting research and publishing in marketing: from conceptualisation through the review process', *Journal of the Academy of Marketing Science*, vol. 29, no. 4, pp. 405–415.

Swales, J 1984, 'Research into the structure of introductions to journal articles and its application to the teaching of academic writing', in *Common Ground: Shared Interests in ESP and Communication Studies*, eds R Williams R & J Swales J, Pergamon, Oxford.

Szymanaski, DM & Henard, DH 2000, 'Customer satisfaction: a meta-analysis of the empirical evidence', *Journal of the Academy of Marketing Science*, vol. 29, no. 1, pp. 16–35.

Taylor, D n.d., 'The literature review: a few tips on conducting it', University of Toronto, viewed 29 November 2012, < http://www.writing.utoronto.ca/advice/specific-types-of-writing/literature-review>.

Taylor, D & Proctor, M 2005, 'The literature review: a few tips on conducting it', University of Toronto, viewed 21 March 2011, <http://www.writing.utoronto.ca/advice/specific-types-of-writing/literature-review>.

The Economist 2007, 'What is the point of research carried out in business schools?', 24 August, viewed 16 May 2008, <Economist.com>.

'The writer's handbook using transitions' 2012, University of Wisconsin-Madison, viewed 6 December 2012, <http://writing.wisc.edu/Handbook/Transitions.html>.

Thomas, G 1977, *Leader Effectiveness Training*, Wyden, New York.

Thompson, F 2003, 'An action research analysis of factors involved in Australian small- to medium-sized enterprises planning and tendering for overseas development aid projects', PhD thesis, Southern Cross University, Gold Coast, Australia.

Thompson, F & Perry, C 2004, 'How can the results of an action research project in one work place be generalised to other situations?', *European Journal of Marketing*, vol. 38, no. 3/4, pp. 401–417.

Thompson, L 2004, *Making the Team: a Guide for Managers*, 2nd edn, Pearson Prentice Hall, Upper Saddle River.

University of Oregon n.d., *General Guidelines for Research Writing*, Oregon Graduate School,University of Oregon, Oregon, based on an original document by the College of Health, Physical Education and Recreation, Pennsylvania State University.

van Wynsberghe, R & Khan, S 2007, 'Redefining case study', *International Journal of Qualitative Methods*, vol. 6, no. 2, pp. 80–94.

Varadarajan, PR 1996, 'From the Editor: reflections on research and publishing', *Journal of Marketing*, vol. 60, October, pp. 3–6, p. 306.

Webster J & Watson RT 2002, 'Analyzing the past to prepare for the future: writing a literature review', *MIS Quarterly*, vol. 26, no. 2, pp. xiii-xxiii.

'What rules determine authorship on publications?' 2011, authororder, viewed 20 october 2012, <http://www.authorder.com/index.php?option=com_content&view=article&id=28&Itemid=47>.

Witcher, B 1990, 'What should a PhD look like?', *Graduate Management Research*, vol. 5, no. 1, pp. 29–36.

'Writing an article' n.d., *ANZ Journal of Surgery*, viewed 29 July 2011, <http://www.anzjsurg.com/view/0/writingAnArticle.html>.

Woodward, T 1996, 'Identifying the measuring customer-based brand equity and its elements for a service industry', PhD thesis, Queensland University of Technology.

Wolcott, HF 1990, *Writing Up Qualitative Research*, Sage, Newbury Park.

Yin, RK 2009, *Case Study Research: Design and Methods*, 4th edn, Sage, London.

Zikmund, WG 2000, *Business Research Methods*, 6th edn, Dryden, Chicago.

Zuber-Skerritt, O (ed.) 1992, *Starting Research—Supervision and Training*, Tertiary Education Institute, University of Queensland, Brisbane.

Zuber-Skerritt, O 2001, 'Action learning and action research: paradigm, praxis and programs', in *Effective Change Management Using Action Research and Action Learning: Concepts, Frameworks, Processes and Applications*, eds S Sankaran, B Dick, R Passfield and P Swepson, Southern Cross University Press, Lismore, Australia, pp. 1–20.

Zuber-Skerritt, O & Knight, N 1992, 'Problem definition and thesis writing', *Higher Education*, vol. 15, no. 1–2, pp. 89–103.

Zuber-Skerritt, O & Knight, N 1992, 'Problem definition and thesis writing—workshops for the postgraduate student', in *Starting Research—Supervision And Training*, ed. O Zuber-Skerritt, Tertiary Education Institute, University of Queensland.

Zuber-Skerritt, O and Perry, C 2002, 'Action research within organisations and university thesis writing', *Organisational Learning*, vol. 9, no. 4, pp. 171–179.

INDEX

A

academic journals
  questions considered by reviewers, 72, 119
  reviewers and anonymity, 90, 92, 95
  role of reviewers, 93, 94, 95
  top tier, 9, 87
  see also writing for journals
action research, iii, iv, 41, 81, 105, 121, 147–73
  core project, 148, 149, 160, 161, 165–7
  criteria for judging quality, 163–4, 165–72
  critical theory and realism paradigms, 150, 155–63. 165–73
  data analysis, 160, 163, 165, 166, 168, 169, 170, 171
  data collection, 157, 158, 160, 165, 168, 170
  definition, 155–6
  examples of projects, 157–8, 162–3
  generalising project, 148, 149, 160, 161, 169–72
  goals, 149
  justification for academic, 162
  methodology, 148
  practical, 158, 159
  report writing, 161–2, 163
  spiral of cycles, 148, 156–7,160
  technical, 158, 159
  two stakeholders, 148–9
  types and characteristics, 159
  validity and reliability, 149, 160
analytical models, 36–7, 38, 40, 61
appendices to theses, 12, 66
  contents, 38, 39, 45, 162

B

Bartlett's tests, 44
bias, 44, 46, 48, 118, 142
business people/managers, iii, 3, 6, 25, 41, 64, 68, 89, 90, 104, 106, 109, 110, 111, 114, 120, 121–2, 148, 152, 158

C

case research, iii, 42, 48, 51, 65, 101–23
  analytic generalisation, 119–20
  comparison with convergent interviewing, 141
  computer-assisted analysis, 115-16
  convergent interviewing, 114–15
  cross–case and cross cluster analysis, 119
  data analysis, 116–19
  data coding, 117

definition, 102
delimitations, 110
embedded cases, 111
ethics, 116
growing importance, 101–2
identifying a case, 109–12
implications, 120–2
interviewing techniques, 115
interviews, 113–16
intrinsic and instrumental, 107
literature review, 108, 114
multiple sources of evidence, 112–16
number of cases, 47, 107, 109–12
number of interviews, 113–14, 115
procedures, 102
realism criteria, 116
realism paradigm, 103–7, 108, 116, 120
replication logic, 111
reporting findings, 118–19
research problem and research issues, 107–9
research quality, 116
seven steps, 107
single case investigation, 110–11
themes, 117–18
theoretical and literal replication, 112
theory building, 122
theory testing, 109, 122
triangulation, 106, 110, 115, 116
chi-square test, 48
citations, 89, 108, 115
counts, 83
  examiners' research, 40
  style, 14, 15, 90, 91
communication
  between supervisors and students, ii, 3, 11
  face-to-face interviews, 131
  journal article quality, 73
  with examiners, 17–18
conclusions and implications (chapter 5 of five-chapter structure for theses), 16, 55–66
  conclusion, 65–6
  conclusions based on findings, 60–1
  example of contribution to knowledge discussion, 58–60
  example of implications for theory section, 63–4
  explanation of findings, 57–60
  limitations and further research, 65
  methodology, 64
  policy and practice, 64
  qualitative findings, 60
  research contribution, 56–7
  theoretical implications, 62–4
conclusions of chapters within five-chapter structure of theses, 32, 49
conferences, 34, 40, 77, 79, 81
  presenting papers, 79
  writing papers, ii, 19, 68, 77
convergent interviewing, iii–iv, 114–15, 125–46
  agreements and disagreements between interviewees, 127–8
  closing the interview, 135
  comparison with alternative methodologies, 139–42
  conceptual framework, 139
  data analysis and interpretation, 135–9, 144
  definition, 126
  ethical conduct, 132
  framework, 128
  initial contact, 120
  Internet research, 131, 136, 137–8

INDEX 195

interview techniques, 133–5
interviewee selection, 129–30
interviewer selection, 131
interviewer's guide, 129
location and duration of interview, 131
number of interviews, 130–1
outcomes, 135–9
purpose, 128
recording, 132
setting up interview, 131–2
snowball technique of interviewee selection, 130, 143
strengths and limitations of technique, 142–3
themes, 135–6
validity and reliability, 143–6
voice recognition software, 132
critical theory paradigm, iv, 103, 105–6, 109, 115–16, 121, 149, 150, 152–4, 155–63, 164, 165–8

D

data analyses (chapter 4 of five-chapter structure for theses), 30, 49–55
   correctness, 45
   computer programs, 48
   p values, 52, 53
   qualitative data, 53–4
   quantitative data, 52–3
   reporting findings, 51–5
   statistical tests, 52–3
   tables and figures, 49–50, 54–5
   see also action research; case research; convergent interviewing
data collection, 11, 27, 30–1, 39, 41, 43–4, 60, 65, 107, 128
   action research, 157, 158, 160, 165, 168, 170

convergent interviewing, 144
focus, 33, 35, 37, 41, 68
instruments/procedures, 48
methodology, 69
quality, 114
records, 45
special treatment of data, 48
unit of analysis, 48
DBAs, 3, 5, 10, 12, 13, 24, 121–2
see also theses
definitions, 30–1, 33, 68
   constructs, operational, 24, 42, 43, 47, 69
delimitations, 6–7, 24, 25, 31–2, 65, 68
   case research, 110
   definition, 32
   see also limitations

E

epistemology, 107, 151
ethics, 48, 49, 116, 132, 133
examination criteria, 72–4
examiners of theses
   citing publications of, 40
   personal preferences of, 31
   previous reports of, 4
   selection of panel of, 17
examiners of theses, information for
   checklist of possible questions, 72–3
   conclusions based on findings, 60–1
   core thesis requirements, 4
   delimitations and justifications, 31
   limitations acknowledged, 65
   methodology, 44, 45, 47, 49
   practical and policy implications, 64
   style note, 15

summary listing of research contribution, 61
university/faculty letter, 4
variables influencing data results, 49
explanatory research, 41, 42–3
exploratory research, 41–2

F

factor analysis, 44
five-chapter structure for theses, 1, 7–8, 163
  justification for using, 9–11
  justified changes, 11–13
  linking chapters, 14
  model, 8
  word count, approximate percentages for each chapter, 11
  see also conclusions and implications; data analyses; introductions; methodologies; research issues
focus groups, 140, 141–2, 157

H

Higher Education Research and Development Society of Australia, 9
honours theses, 3, 47

I

interpretive paradigms, 16, 48, 105–6, 116
interview research, 113–16, 125–46

dates, 45, 49
in-depth interviews, 126, 133, 139, 140, 141
interviewee quotations, 42, 118, 119
interviewing techniques, 115
number of interviews, 47, 113–14, 115
protocols, 49
recording interviews, 46, 115, 132, 133, 135, 142
see also convergent interviewing
introductions (chapter 1 of five-chapter structure for theses), 22–32
  contribution to literature, 27–8, 34, 56–61
  definitions, 30–1
  delimitations, 31–2
  justification for research, 29–30
  methodology, 30
  research background, 22–3
  research issues, 26–7
  research problem/hypothesis, 23–8
introductions to chapters within five-chapter structure for theses, 7, 14, 54, 56

J

journal articles
see academic journals; writing articles for journals

L

Likert scale, 16, 44–5
limitations, 32, 48, 65
　see also delimitations
literature reviews, 23, 32–43
　case research, 108, 114
　journal articles, 89
　preliminary, 68
　summary table, 39–40
　see also research issues

M

Master's theses, 10, 23, 47
methodologies (chapter 3 of five-chapter structure for theses), iii, 30, 43–9
　body of knowledge about, 44
　evidence about assumptions, 48
　evidence of correct procedures, 45
　justifications, 30, 47–8
　limitations, 48
　operational definitions, 47
　precise details, 47–8
　use of personal pronoun 'I', 16, 42, 46
　validity and reliability, 44, 46, 47, 48
　variables, 49
　see also action research; case research; interview research

N

neuroscience, 105

O

ontology, 107, 150

P

paradigms, iv, 26, 27, 46, 103–7, 149
　constructivism, 103, 104, 105, 107, 109, 115, 121, 152–4
　critical theory, iv, 103, 105–6, 109, 115–16, 121, 149, 150, 152–4, 155–63, 164, 165–8
　diagrams illustrating, 104, 150–1
　interpretivism, 16, 48, 105–6, 116
　positivism, 48, 65, 103–5, 106, 108, 116, 122, 150, 151, 152
　realism, iv, 102, 103, 104, 106–7, 108, 116, 120, 149, 150, 154–5, 155–63, 164, 159–72
parent theories, 6, 10, 27, 33, 34–5, 43, 60, 62, 63, 68, 77–8
　classification models, 36–7, 40, 61
　examples of, 39
personal contribution/opinion/perception of researcher, 16, 32–3, 38, 107
　bias, 46, 118, 142
　literature review, 36, 37, 40
　use of personal pronoun 'I', 16, 42, 46
pilot studies, 44, 47, 48, 70, 131
PowerPoint presentations, 79
practical problem solving, iii, 64, 149, 158
　see also action research; case research; convergent interviewing
propositions/hypotheses
　see research issues

Q

qualitative research, iii, 41–2, 43, 44, 51, 53–4, 61, 109, 114, 118, 125, 139, 141, 142, 147
  aspects of unified thesis, 46
  quality of research, 19, 73, 86, 111, 114, 116, 142, 149, 160, 163–4, 165–73
  see also validity and reliability
quantitative research, 42–3, 51, 52–3, 103, 109, 112–13, 120, 143, 147
  aspects of unified thesis, 46
quotations, 29, 40, 42, 53, 54, 86, 89, 117, 118, 119, 139, 157, 170
  length, 40
  style, 14, 15, 16, 88-90

R

realism paradigm, iv, 102
real-world, iii, 102, 108, 122, 152, 157, 170
records, 45, 145, 157
references, 12, 16, 19, 40, 44, 48, 51, 57, 66, 67, 69, 72, 81, 91, 108, 115
  of examiners, 40
  style, 14, 15, 40, 90
regression analysis, 30, 42, 44, 49
replication studies, 152
research colleagues, ii, 19, 75, 76, 77, 79, 91, 81, 87, 91, 92, 95, 96
research contribution, 27–8, 34, 56–61
  applying existing instrument in new application, 47
  applying existing theory in new setting, 28
  example discussion, 59–60
  justification, 29–30
  literature/body of knowledge, 27, 34, 55, 56–61
  summary listing, 61
research 'gaps', 7, 22, 25, 29, 35, 37, 38, 43, 59, 67, 68, 78, 81, 82, 84, 85, 88, 89, 108, 160
research issues (chapter 2 of five-chapter structure for theses), 26–7, 32–43, 49
  classification models of parent theories, 36–7
  context of research, 38–9
  pathways guiding data collection and analysis, 41–3
  research problem theory and parent theories, 33–5
  summary table of literature, 39–40
research problem/unifying hypothesis, 9, 22, 23–8
  conceptual framework, 24, 32–3, 34, 37, 61, 62, 68
  context of research, 24, 38–9
  delimitations, 24, 25, 31–2, 65, 68
  identification, 25
  Master's thesis, 23
  PhD thesis, 24
  solution, 26, 27, 87
  theory, 15, 33, 34–5, 36, 37
research proposals, 66–70
  contribution to knowledge, 67–8
  length, 66
  references, 67
  research methods, 69
  research topic and justification, 67
  resources, 70
  thesis outline and timetable, 69–70

S

scree tests, 44
significance tests, 49, 50, 53
structural equation modelling, 44, 61, 139
structured approach
  see five-chapter structure for theses
style, 14–20, 43–4
  citations and references, 14, 15, 40, 90
  communication with examiners, 17–18
  conclusions about research issues, 57
  first person pronoun, 16, 42, 46
  journal articles, 15, 16, 88–90
  justification for decisions/claims, 16–17
  note for examiners, 15
  past/present tense, 16, 45
  quotations, 14
  style manuals, 14–15
  tables and figures, 50, 55
  tone, 16
supervisors
  communicating with students, 11
  deciding on panel of examiners, 17
  number of, 19–20
  provision of previous examiners' reports, 4
  reviewing thesis drafts, 19–20
surveys, 16, 30, 38, 39, 42, 43, 44, 45, 46, 47, 48, 51, 52, 65, 70, 103, 112, 113, 120, 121, 139, 147, 151, 157
  (non-)response bias, 44, 48
  sample, 30, 44, 113

T

tables and figures, 12, 15, 49–50, 54–5
tables of contents, structured thesis example, 5–6
theses
  action research projects, 163
  adapting parts for conferences and journals, 19
  'chunkiness', 20–2
  completion times, ii, 10, 12, 13
  criteria for judging, 4
  see also writing theses

U

universities, i, 4, 10, 34, 45, 75, 87
  choice of examiners, 17
  letter to examiners, 4
  research proposal requirements, 66
  style requirements, 14–15, 19
  word count requirements, 11
University of New South Wales, 28
University of Queensland, 11

V

validity and reliability, 44, 46, 47, 48, 113, 116, 125, 143–6, 149
  construct validity, 110, 116, 145
  external validity, 48, 90, 119, 120, 145
  internal validity, 48, 90, 145
  reliability, 145
  tests for 144
Vancouver protocol, 82

W

Wilcoxon test, 48
writing articles for journals, 49, 75–96
  abstracts, 76, 79, 80, 81, 84
  action research projects, 163
  backup journal, 76, 78, 95, 96
  case research, 118
  citations and references, 90
  co-authors/collaborators, ii, 19, 81, 95
  completion times, ii, 75, 96
  conceptual framework, 85, 89
  conclusions, 87, 90
  contact with editors, 92, 93, 94
  contribution to conversation, 77, 83, 85, 86, 95
  contribution importance, 86–7
  data analysis, 90
  detailed steps, 76
  drafting stages, 91
  empirical articles, 86
  first draft of an article, 88
  getting cited, 83–4, 87
  headings, 9, 88
  introductions, 85
  keywords, 83–4
  linkages with theses, 10, 56, 77, 90
  literature reviews, 89
  methodology, 89–90
  p values, 53
  portfolio of articles-in-progress, 78–9
  quotations, 89
  redrafting, 91–6
  rejection, 95, 96
  reviewers, 93–4, 95
  structure/table of contents, 88
  style, 15, 16, 88–90
  submitting, 92–3
  target journal, 80, 96
  team planning synopsis, 82
  themes, 118
  theory building/literature review articles, 85, 86
  titles, 83–4
  universal contribution, 87
  backup journal, 76, 78, 95, 96
  word limits, 80, 84, 119
  see also academic journals; journal articles
writing theses, 3–73
  appendices, 12, 38, 39, 45, 162
  drafts, 19–20
  linking chapters, 14, 20
  linking paragraphs, 20
  numbering sections, 9
  overall structure, 7–14
  openness, 26, 30
  order of, 27
  page layout and typeface, 12, 19
  tables of contents, 5–6
  themes, 118
  word count, approximate percentages for each chapter, 11–13
  word count requirements of universities, 11
  see also conclusions and implications; data analyses; five-chapter structure for theses; introductions; methodologies; research issues; style

OTHER BOOKS FROM AIB PUBLICATIONS

WORK-APPLIED LEARNING FOR CHANGE

The book will be of special value for Chief Executives and other senior managers who are responsible for change in their organisations, as well as academics in institutions with a teaching and research interest in this field.

This new release from AIB Publications is available now in paperback from all good online stockists. AIB Publications specialises in management, business and research texts and is the publishing arm of the Australian Institute of Business.

"Far from the aggressive and manipulative command and control mentality of so much management 'advice', the WAL approach humanises the process of change management. It takes people into account, not just as variables in the equation, but as stakeholders and learners whose participation and work-applied learning is critical to achieving the benefits of change.

This book should not be easily dismissed by the more traditionally-minded management scholars, as it stands on its own, with substantial academic merit, but more importantly, with demonstrable real-world application. It's a good book. I really do recommend it."

Paul Davidson
Associate Professor of Management,
Queensland University of Technology - Business School

"I welcome this book. As Selva Abraham acknowledges (p. 6), there are many views on the meaning and method of implementation of Action Learning and Action Research. The Work-Applied Learning (WAL) model is an interesting example of going beyond the discussion of these variations and using a fused model to extract the most from the intervention for the client organisation. The "wheels within the wheels" of the mini-cycles within major cycles produces a highly flexible approach that creates learning for individuals, organisational learning, and rigour in the intervention."

Colin Bradley
President
Action Learning, Action Research Association Inc.
www.alara.net.au

Printed in Australia
AUOC01n1120260713
257144AU00003B/1/P